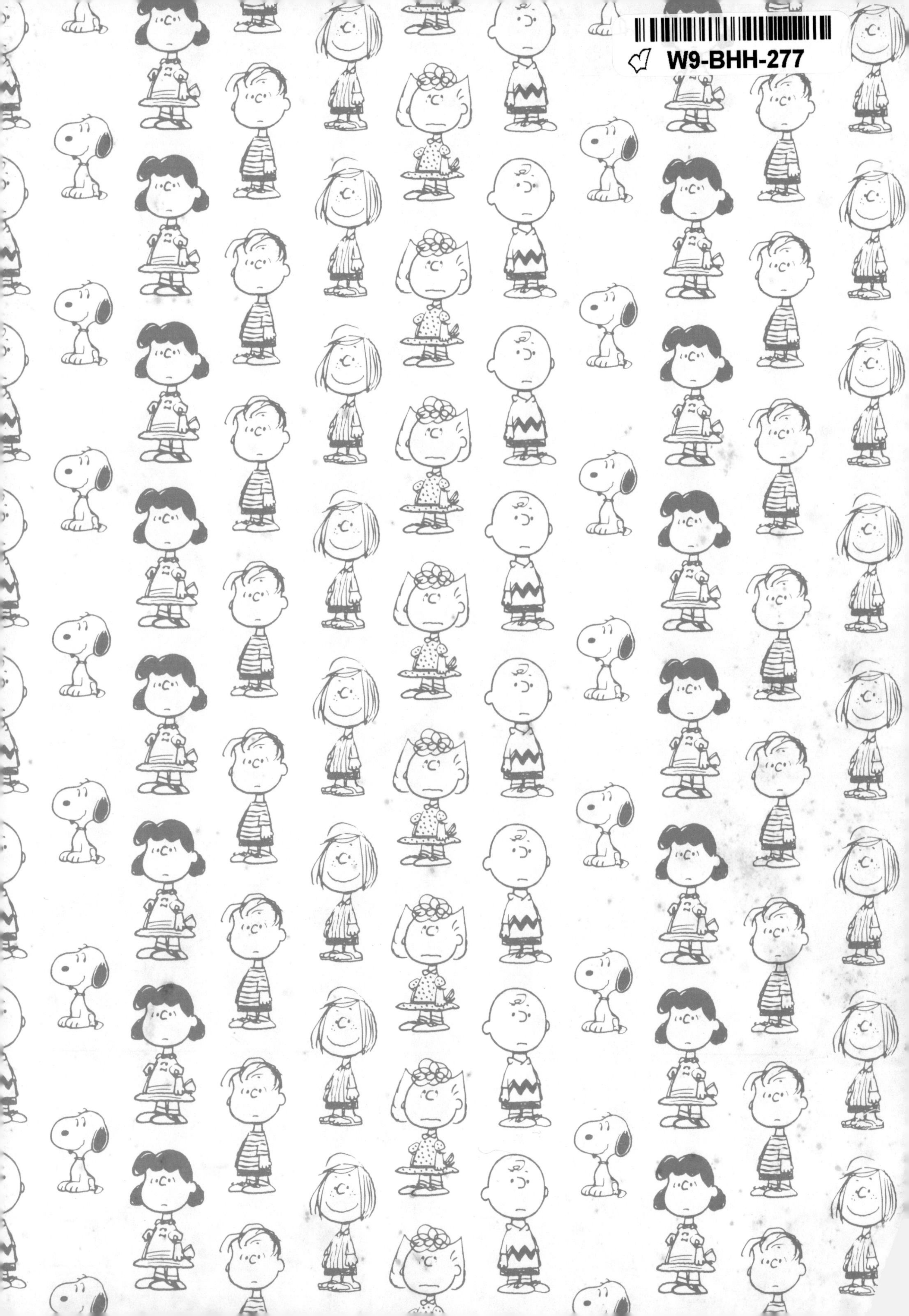

WELCOME TO SNOOPY'S WORLD

PEOPLE AND CUSTOMS OF THE WORLD

Based on the Characters of Charles M. Schulz

Derrydale Books
New York • Avenel

Based on the English Language Book "CHARLIE BROWN'S
'CYCLOPEDIA—VOLUMES 12, 14, 11" © 1990 United Feature Syndicate, Inc.

This 1994 edition is published by Derrydale Books,
distributed by Random House Value Publishing, Inc.,
40 Engelhard Avenue, Avenel, New Jersey 07001

Cover designed by Bill Akunevicz Jr.
Production supervised by Roméo Enriquez

Manufactured in the United States of America

Library of Congress Cataloging-in-Publication Data
Schulz, Charles M.
People and customs of the world / Illustrated by Charles Schulz.
p.   cm.—(Snoopy's world)
ISBN 0-517-11895-5
1. Costume—Juvenile literature. 2. Holidays—Juvenile literature.
3. Ethnology—Juvenile literature. [1. Costume. 2. Holidays. 3. Ethnology.]
I. Title. II. Series: Schulz, Charles M. Snoopy's world.
GT518.S38   1994
390—dc20
94-13723
CIP   AC

10 9 8 7 6 5 4 3 2 1

INTRODUCTION

In *People and Customs of the World*, you'll discover new lands, unusual holidays, and people from faraway places. Have you ever wondered why queens wear crowns, or how the Eskimos keep warm, or how trick-or-treating got started? Charlie Brown, Snoopy, and the rest of the *Peanuts* gang are here to help you find the answers to these questions and many more about people and their customs all over the world. Have fun!

CONTENTS

CONTENTS

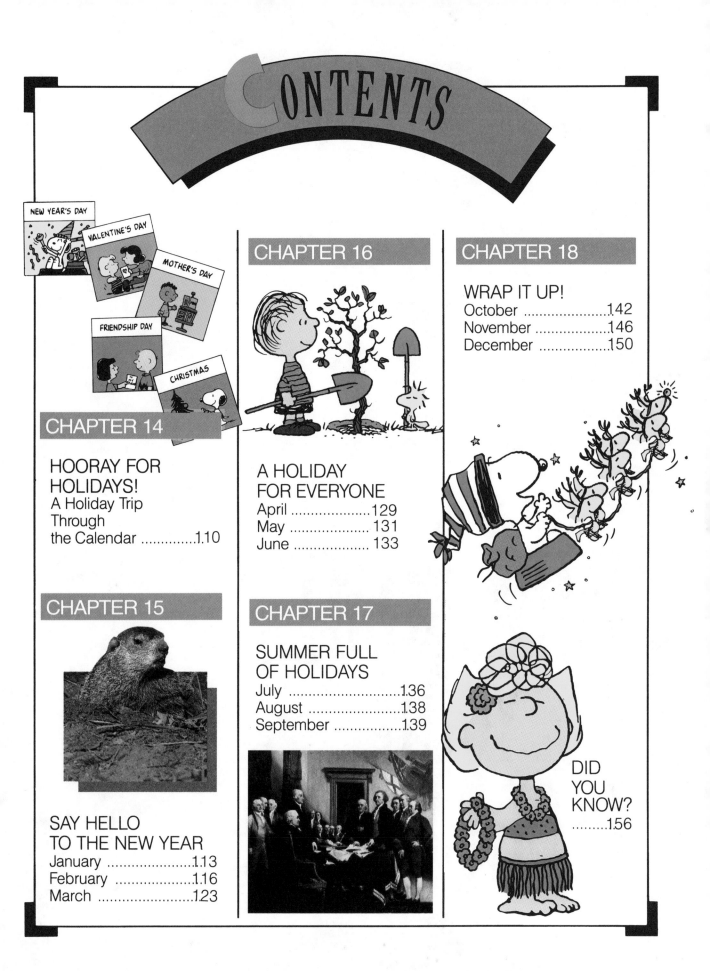

CONTENTS

When early explorers took to the seas, they made an amazing discovery. The Earth wasn't flat, as they all had thought. It was round! Since then, the Earth has been mapped out by sailors, pilots, and astronauts. Climb aboard Linus's magic blanket, and you, too, can travel around the world with the *Peanut's* gang!

WELCOME TO YOUR WORLD

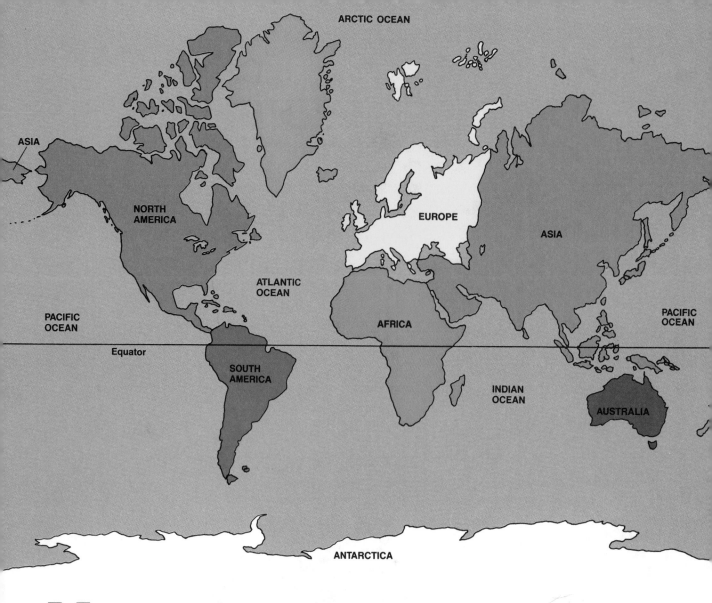

CHAPTER 1

MAPPING OUT THE CONTINENTS

Which continent do you live on?

Look at the map above. Can you find the continent you live on? If you live in the United States, you are on the continent of North America.
If you live in Japan, you are in Asia. If England is your home, your continent is Europe.

What is a continent?

A continent is a large mass of land. Earth has seven continents: Africa, Antarctica, Asia, Australia, Europe, North America, and South America.

What is a map used for?

A map is a drawing that shows an area, usually on the surface of the Earth. Maps tell us about the size and location of land, bodies of water, mountains, and deserts. Maps help travelers find their way. Bodies of water usually appear as blue areas. Can you find the ocean on this map?

THE EQUATOR AND ANTARCTICA

Why is there a line across the center of the map?

The line across the center of the map is the equator. This line divides the world in half. The part of the world above the line is called the Northern Hemisphere. The part under the line is called the Southern Hemisphere. If you traveled to the equator, you would not see an actual line, but you would encounter very hot weather. The equator is the warmest part of the Earth because it receives the Sun's rays most directly.

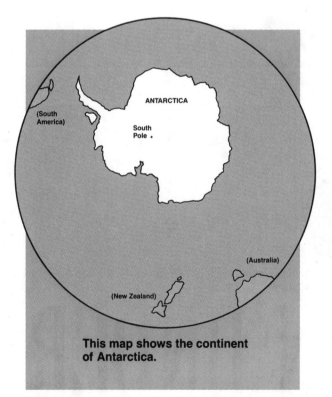

This map shows the continent of Antarctica.

What is the coldest continent?

Antarctica, which some people call the South Pole, is the coldest continent. It is almost completely covered with ice. In some places, the ice is two miles thick. Ninety-five percent of the ice in the world can be found in Antarctica. One Antarctic iceberg was thought to be the size of Belgium, a small country in Europe!

It is so cold in Antarctica that no tree or bush can grow. Scientists visit Antarctica to study it, but they don't stay very long. The only animals there are penguins, birds, and seals. They eat food from the sea.

CHAPTER 2

AUSTRALIA

Our next stop is the world's smallest continent—Australia. It is also the Earth's largest island. This continent has just one country, and that country has the same name as the continent—Australia. Grab your bag, and follow Charlie Brown to the land down under, mate!

DOWN UNDER

THE OUTBACK WILDERNESS

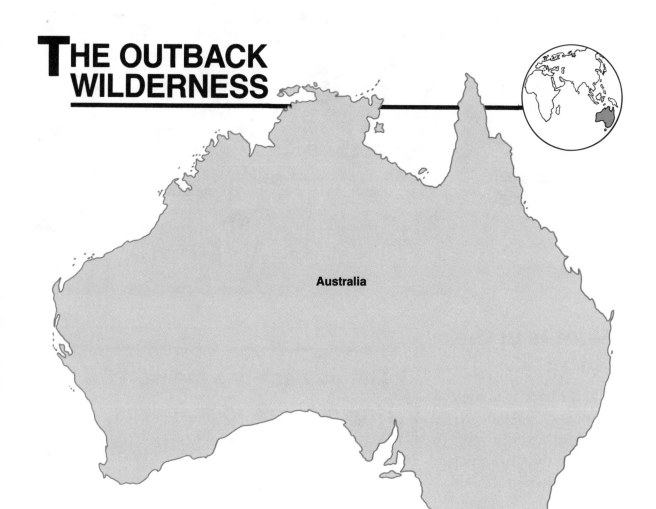

Australia

Why is Australia called the land down under?

Except for Antarctica, Australia is the only continent that is totally south of the equator. Because most of Australia's settlers came from north of the equator, they called it "the land down under."

What is the continent of Australia like?

Most of the people in Australia live in cities around the edge of the island. These cities were built near the water because seaports make cities easy to reach by boat. The land in Australia that doesn't border the ocean is called the outback.

13

Ayers Rock, found in the Australian outback, is the largest rock in the world.

What is in the outback?

The outback is made up of plains and plateaus—flat land without any trees. Some of the people who live in the outback are sheep or cattle ranchers. Outback ranches are so big that people are very far away from their nearest neighbor. They don't even have telephones! People use two-way radios to talk to their friends.

The outback has the world's largest single rock. It rises about 1,000 feet. The top is almost completely round because of erosion!

IF WE WENT TO SCHOOL IN AUSTRALIA, WE WOULDN'T HAVE TO WAIT FOR A STUPID SCHOOL BUS!

How do children go to school in the outback?

Outback children don't "go" to school. They learn their lessons right in their own homes. Their teachers talk to them over the same radio that the people use for talking to neighbors. This school is called School of the Air. Its students must mail their homework and tests to their teachers.

THE BIG CITIES

What do Australian cities look like?

Australian cities look like other big cities in the world. They have some tall office buildings, crowded city streets, and lots of people. Australian cities are a little different, though. They usually are very spread out, with houses instead of apartment buildings. Most Australians like to own their own homes.

What are the city schools like?

They are similar to schools in the United States. Students must go to school from age 6 to 16. Australia also has colleges and universities.

What do city dwellers in Australia do for fun?

Sports are very important to Australians. There are many young people in Australia, and young people usually like to play sports. The weather is warm much of the year, so most sports can be played year round.

Because most of the cities are near water, water sports are very popular. Australians like to swim, sail, fish, and water-ski. Tennis and golf are also popular. Many British games, such as cricket, also are played. Cricket is similar to baseball, but players use a stick called a wicket to hit the ball.

What language do Australians speak?

English is the official language of Australia because the land was settled by people from England. The Australian accent is closer to an English accent than it is to an American accent, but it is still different. Australians also have some different words. Sometimes it is hard for Americans and British people to understand what Australians are talking about even though the Australians are speaking English!

Australian Word	Meaning
jumbuck	sheep
shivoo	party
mate	friend
plonk	wine
willy-willy	windstorm
drongo	fool

C'MON, MATE! WE'VE BEEN INVITED TO A SHIVOO AT CHUCK'S.

PRISONERS AND ABORIGINES

Why did the English settlers move to Australia?

In the 1700s, the jails in England were very crowded. The British people didn't know what to do with all the prisoners. Many of them were in jail just because they disagreed with the king. They weren't dangerous. The English government decided to clean out the jails by sending some of these prisoners to live in Australia.

Were people already living in Australia when the settlers arrived?

Yes, there were people called aborigines. Their life-style was different from that of the new settlers. Many of the aborigines were nomads, people who move from place to place. Although the aborigines had home bases to which they always returned, they were often on the move.

The aborigines invented the boomerang, a flat, curved object that turns in flight and comes back to the thrower!

Are there any aborigines in Australia today?

Yes. Some still live a nomadic life, as their ancestors did. Although they travel, most aborigines have home bases to which they return. Others moved to reservations similar to those in the United States. Many aborigines have moved to the big cities to live side by side with other Australians.

Who else moved to Australia besides the prisoners?

In the mid-1800s, gold was discovered in Australia. Many people came from all over the world, wanting to get rich. Most of these settlers came from England, but some also came from the Americas and China.

Even now, Australians want people to move to their continent. The country has large amounts of empty land available for new settlers. In the past 40 years, two million people have moved to Australia. They are called "new" people.

One out of every six people in Australia is a "new" person!

A woman strips the leaves of a palm tree for weaving.

A spear is made with the help of an open fire.

This aboriginal man is playing a didjeridu (did-you-ree-DEW), a musical instrument that is similar to a flute.

CHAPTER 3

THE SECRETS OF ASIA

I f you head north from Australia, you'll be in Asia, the world's largest continent. You will see snowy mountains and rice-growing lowlands, skyscrapers in big cities and deserts in remote places, beautiful green islands and forever-icy plains. And you'll see millions of fascinating people along the way. All aboard for Asia!

MOUNT EVEREST

THE COUNTRIES OF ASIA

Which countries are on the continent of Asia?

Many countries make up Asia. From the vastness of the independent Slavic states and Russia to the South Pacific islands, Asia is a land of tremendous variety.

Charlie Brown is going to show you how people live in two fascinating places in Asia, the highest places and the lowest places.

THE HIMALAYAN FAMILIES

What are the Himalayas?

The Himalayas (him-uh-LAY-uhz) are a huge mountain chain in the southern part of Asia. These mountains stretch across three entire countries—Nepal (nuh-PAWL), Sikkim (SICK-im), and Bhutan (boo-TAHN). The Himalayas also touch parts of India, Pakistan, and Tibet. Although the Himalayan people live in different countries, they are alike in many ways.

19

What is the tallest mountain in the world?

Mount Everest, in the Himalayas, is the tallest. It is 5½ miles high! That's almost 20 times as tall as the Empire State Building in New York City. There are 92 peaks in the Himalayas that are more than four miles high.

The highest mountains in the Himalayas get most of their heavy snows in the summer!

Himalayan houses in Nepal

Who lives in the Himalayas?

About 20 million people live there. They have dark, straight hair, dark eyes, and brown skin. Himalayan people are short, but they are strong.

Most people of the Himalayas live in small villages on the narrow strips of land between high mountains. We call these flat, narrow places valleys.

What are Himalayan houses like?

Most are made of stone. Because glass is expensive, there are few windows. The houses also stay warmer without windows. Some houses have flat roofs. Others have roofs with a slight slant. Himalayan people lay heavy stones on top of both kinds of roofs. The stones keep the roofs from blowing off in the strong mountain winds that blow all the time.

Himalayan houses are small, but they have two or three floors. The third floor is used to store food and hay. More food and wood are stored on the ground floor, which also becomes a barn for animals in the winter. The second floor of the house has one big room where the family lives.

In cold weather, the family gathers around an open fire. The fire keeps them warm and cooks their food.

TIBETAN YAK

Which animal is the best friend of the Himalayan people?

The yak, a big animal that looks like a buffalo, is their best friend. Because yaks can live in rugged mountain areas, they are used for many purposes.

Yaks supply people with meat and milk. They also pull plows for Himalayan farmers, carry heavy loads, and can be ridden like horses. Mountain women weave the yaks' long hair into cloth for blankets and clothing. Yak hide makes warm, sturdy boots.

Even the yaks' horns are useful. They are made into musical instruments.

While looking for grass to eat, yaks have climbed close to the top of Mount Everest!

How do Himalayan people earn a living?

Some raise sheep, goats, or yaks. A few work as guides for tourists and mountain climbers, but most are farmers. They raise cereal crops such as barley and wheat on the mountain slopes. Himalayan people also grow fruits and vegetables in the valleys near their homes.

What do Himalayan people eat?

These mountain people eat the cereal and other crops that they raise. Barley, for example, is roasted, then ground, and made into bread. Boiled or fried potatoes are a favorite food.

Yak meat, a treat to Himalayan people, is eaten fresh, or after it has been dried. However, people don't have it often because they like to keep their yaks alive as long as possible. Yaks are killed for meat only when they are quite old. Yak meat is a nice change from sheep and goat meat, which the people eat more often. Himalayan people drink yak milk, and make cheese and butter from it. They also drink tea to which salt and yak butter are added.

These Himalayan children attend school in the local village.

Do Himalayan villages have stores?

Most Himalayan villages do not have stores. Families grow or make the things they need.

Once a year, a Himalayan family travels to a market town. There, people from all over the mountain area gather to buy and sell goods. Some markets are held outdoors.

Family members take with them the sweaters, blankets, and other things they have made. At the market, they trade for whatever they need: tea, spices, or metal tools. Because they trade one thing for another, many mountain people do not use money.

Do Himalayan children go to school?

Some do, and some don't. Only large villages and towns have schools. The mountains make it impossible for children to travel back and forth from one village to another every day. Children from small villages have to leave home for a while to go to school, but not very many do. For that reason a lot of children never learn to read and write. Instead, they learn to plant crops, weave, cook, and do other practical jobs. Children from large towns learn reading, writing, and arithmetic, and some go on to college in other countries.

What do Himalayan people do if they get sick?

Many Himalayan people believe that illness is caused by evil spirits. When these people are ill, they call in a shaman (SHAH-man), an important person who is believed to be able to heal sick people. The shaman tries to cure sickness by dealing with spirits, and by using natural medicines.

For a long time, scientists didn't believe a shaman could really cure a sick person. Doctors have learned, however, that shamans use many plants that are in our medicines.

Many Himalayan people who live in small isolated villages never visit a modern doctor. As a result, some of them die of diseases a modern doctor could cure.

COULD IT BE... ABOMINABLE SNOWMEN?

What is the abominable snowman?

There have been many reports of a shaggy creature, called the abominable snowman, who supposedly lives in the Himalayas. Nobody knows for sure if it really exists, but it is reported to be half human and half ape. Some people say it has a high-pitched scream, a bad smell, and feet that point backward. The Himalayan people's word for the abominable snowman is *yeti* (YET-ee).

The mysterious *yeti* is said to roam the Himalayas at night, but few people can prove that they have ever seen the creature. Others claim that they have seen *yeti* tracks in the snow, but no one has ever proved that a *yeti* made the tracks.

23

RICE FARMING IN ASIA'S LOWLANDS

What are the lowlands?

The lowlands are the flat, warm areas of Asia below the mountains and on the coast. In Asia, most of the people live in the lowlands.

Rice fields in the lowlands of Indonesia.

SOMETIMES YOU JUST HAVE TO GET YOUR FEET WET.

Where does rice grow?

Rice, the most commonly eaten food in the world, grows in places that are warm, wet, and, usually, low. More rice is grown in Asia than anywhere else. China, India, Indonesia (in-duh-NEE-zhuh), Bangladesh (BANG-luh-desh), Japan, and Thailand (TIE-land) are the six Asian countries that grow the most rice.

Do many people live in the six main rice-growing countries of Asia?

Yes. Nearly two billion people live there. This is slightly less than half the people in the world! The number of people in these countries is growing very fast. In some areas there, people are already terribly crowded.

How can people find enough land to farm in such crowded places?

Most of Asia's rice growers farm small pieces of land. The land on which rice grows is called a paddy. Some paddies are no bigger than a football field, but there are many of these small paddies. Together they produce a lot of rice. The six main rice-growing countries of Asia produce about 260 million tons of rice a year.

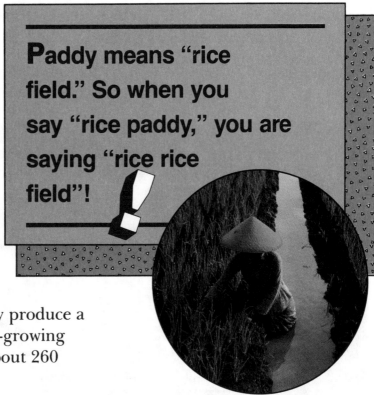

Paddy means "rice field." So when you say "rice paddy," you are saying "rice rice field"!

Which animal helps Asians grow rice?

The water buffalo does. It is a large, strong animal with big horns. In spite of its size, the water buffalo is a gentle animal. A child can safely lead one through the fields.

When a rice farmer plows his paddy, a water buffalo usually pulls the plow. The plow makes ditches in the earth. Then rice seeds are planted in the ditches. From the seeds, stalks grow a few feet high. On the stalks grow the grains that people eat. When the grains are ripe, the stalks are cut down and put on a cart pulled by a water buffalo. The stalks are then spread on the ground. The water buffalo walks over them, forcing the grains off the stalks.

Do rice farmers use any farm machines?

Most paddies are too small for the rice farmer to use farm machines. Instead the work is done by hand. All the family members help to plant the rice and pull weeds from the paddy. When the rice is ripe, they cut it with sharp knives.

Some rice farmers, however, have begun using tractors to pull their plows.

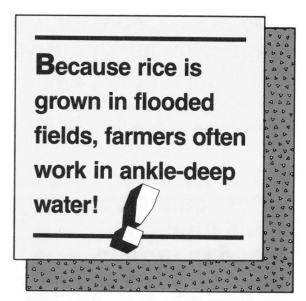

Because rice is grown in flooded fields, farmers often work in ankle-deep water!

Asian rice farmers build their houses on stilts to keep them from being flooded.

Where do rice farmers build their houses?

Rice farmers build their houses in villages. They do not live right next to their fields, as American farmers do. Each morning, the rice farmers walk from the village to their paddies. At the end of the day, they walk back home.

In some rice-growing areas, there are few roads. Rivers and canals go to more places than roads do, so the people usually travel in rowboats and canoes.

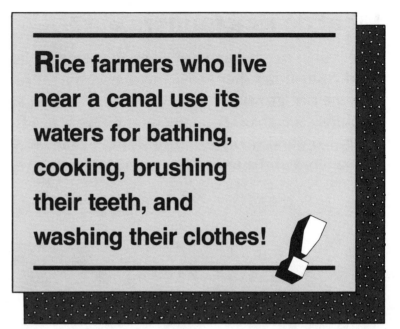

Rice farmers who live near a canal use its waters for bathing, cooking, brushing their teeth, and washing their clothes!

IMAGINE...NO READING, WRITING, OR ARITHMETIC! SOME KIDS HAVE ALL THE LUCK!

Are there schools for rice farmers' children?

There are schools only in some places. In China and Japan, there are schools for the children of all rice-farming families. In other countries, only the largest villages have schools. In some places, teachers visit middle-sized villages for a few months at a time. They teach children to read, write, and do arithmetic, but many children who grow up in small, poor villages never learn to read and write.

27

What do rice farmers eat?

Rice! Asian rice farmers usually boil their rice, but they also eat it steamed or fried. Sometimes they cover the rice with a sauce made from boiled fish.

Some rice-growing families also raise and eat sweet potatoes, beans, peas, or other vegetables. A family might have a few fruit trees, some chickens, and a pig. Now and then, they go fishing, or they buy a fish, but the poorest rice farmers have little to eat besides rice.

Where do rice farmers go shopping?

In the nearest town. Few small villages have stores of their own. For some rice-growing families, going shopping means taking a boat ride on a river or a canal. Other families walk a few miles. In some places, they can ride part of the way in a small bus. Families often take along something to sell at the town market.

Some markets are on water. Here, pots are offered for sale.

Do rice farmers' villages have doctors?

Most villages do not have doctors. A family of rice farmers may live their whole lives without ever visiting a doctor, but some are visited by a shaman. Many of Asia's rice farmers believe that they are surrounded by spirits. They think that spirits live in every field and every house. To these rice farmers, illness means that someone has upset the spirits. When someone is sick, the rice farmers do what the Himalayan people do. They call in a shaman, who tells the sick person how to bring back harmony with the spirits.

CHAPTER 4

From the vineyards of France to the busy streets of London, England and Madrid, Spain; from the fishing villages of Greece to the art museums of Italy; from mountain chalets in Switzerland to rolling farmlands in Poland and centers of industry in Germany—every country in Europe is special, but one is like no other. It's the Netherlands. So take a ride on Woodstock's windmill to this special place.

WINDMILLS OF EUROPE

THE COUNTRIES OF EUROPE

What countries are in the continent of Europe?

This map shows you all the countries in Europe. Some European countries such as Monaco are smaller than many cities in the United States, while others are the size of some of our states. You'll find warm weather in the southern regions of Spain and boot-shaped Italy. In northern Finland and Norway, however, there's so much snow, you'll need a sled to get around!

THE NETHERLANDS

Why is the Netherlands unusual?

The Netherlands, often called Holland, has many rivers, but no mountains. Much of this country is situated below sea level. This means that the land is lower than the level of the sea. The word *netherland* means "low land."

Are there any farms in the Netherlands?

Dutch farms are called *polders*. A *polder* is a section of land that was once underwater. Dutch *polders* are used for growing grain, potatoes, beets, and tulips. Dutch farmers also raise cows. More than half of this country is farmland.

Windmills in the Netherlands

How is water kept out of the *polders*?

The Dutch have built many high walls called dikes to hold back the water from the land. Rain and groundwater are removed with pumps, which are at work all the time. These pumps were once run by windmills, but now they are powered by electricity. Although they are not used as much as in the past, windmills still dot the countryside.

Do the dikes ever break?

Most farmers keep a very close watch on the dikes to make sure they don't break. Storks help the farmers, too! These birds eat small animals that dig into the dike walls to make homes.

Dikes hold back the sea and protect the land in the Netherlands.

Are floods a problem?

Yes. Floods bring a lot of water that presses against the dikes. Sandbags and mats made from tree branches are used to make the dikes stronger.

During wars, the Dutch occasionally opened the seawalls to flood out invaders!

HOW THE DUTCH LIVE

What do the Dutch people do for a living?

As in many places in Europe, some Dutch people work in the tourist business. A lot of other people work in manufacturing. All the rivers and the sea make the Netherlands a good place for trade. Boats can travel by river into the rest of Europe and out into the ocean very easily. Many Dutch people are expert sailors.

What do Dutch farmhouses look like?

A Dutch farmhouse is a house and a barn all in one. The part people live in looks a lot like an American home. In the barn, there are stalls for the cows, and a room for cheese-making. The Dutch produce a lot of cheese and other milk products.

NO, I DIDN'T LOSE MY SANDALS.

?

What do Dutch people wear?

Dutch people wear clothes like those worn in the United States and Europe. Dutch farmers, though, do like to wear wooden shoes. These shoes are good for walking in the wet *polders*. Leather shoes would fall apart quickly.

33

Wax-covered cheese is sold at an open market in the Netherlands.

Do Dutch people go shopping?

Yes. There are many shops and stores in the Netherlands. When the weather is nice, there are open markets in the main squares of some Dutch towns. Shoppers can buy tulips, vegetables, and delicious, creamy cheeses made in the Netherlands.

How do Dutch people travel through their country?

The many canals and rivers make boat travel easy, but the most popular way to travel is by bicycle. The land is very flat, so biking is easy. Biking is also economical, since gas for cars is expensive.

Do Dutch children go to school?

All Dutch children from 6 to 16 years of age attend school. Students attend a primary school for six years. After that, they may attend different types of secondary schools. Some secondary schools prepare students for college. Many of these students will go on to study medicine or science. Some secondary schools help train students for jobs as carpenters, electricians, or secretaries. There are special secondary schools just to teach teachers.

CHAPTER 5

THE DARK CONTINENT OF AFRICA

Some of Africa is covered by desert or tropical jungles, and throughout Africa, there are many big cities. Most of the continent, however, is savannah—open grassland with a few trees. Because of its rough and unfamiliar terrain, travelers in the nineteenth century found it hard to explore Africa. Since no one knew much about this country, it was nicknamed the "dark continent."

THE COUNTRIES OF AFRICA

Which countries are in the continent of Africa?

Many countries are on the large continent of Africa, and no other continent has as many different groups of people. There are Berbers who live in the mountains and deserts of the north, and Kung Bushman hunters who roam the southwest. Tall Masai warriors live in the eastern lands of Kenya and Tanzania, and the Ashanti, whose beautiful sculpture has inspired many American and European artists, live in the west, on the Guinea Coast. The world's oldest civilization was born on the continent of Africa, along the great Nile River in the country of Egypt. We will visit some of the interesting people who call Africa home.

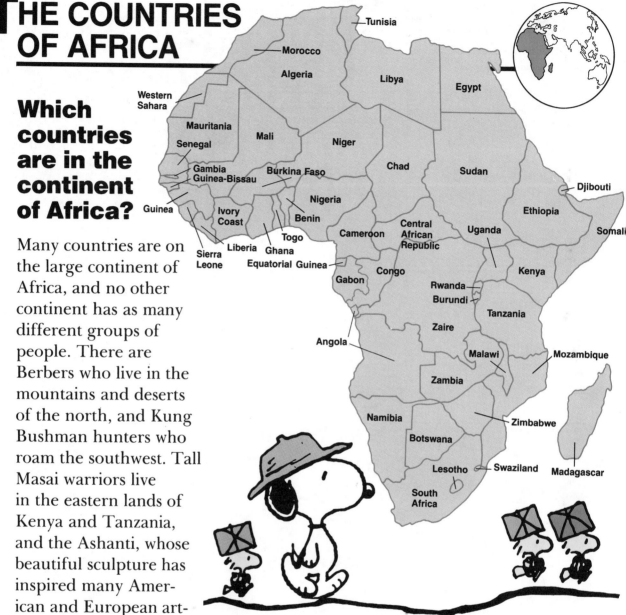

AFRICAN PYGMIES

Who lives in the jungles of central Africa?

Many different groups of people, often called tribes, live there. The largest race of people there are called African pygmies. Most pygmies are short—less than five feet tall.

36

How do pygmies get food?

Most pygmy men are hunters. Women gather fruits and roots. They also fish. Sometimes pygmies trade their meat with nearby farmers in exchange for vegetables.

Pygmies use bows and arrows and spears for hunting. If they are hunting an animal that is very fast and might escape, they put poison on the tips of their arrows and spears. Pygmies also use nets to capture animals before they are killed for food. All of the families make nets, which are tied together. Then the animals are driven into the nets. All animals captured for food are shared by everyone.

Do pygmies always share food?

Yes, they share because pygmies believe in working together. If there is an argument between two people, the tribe gets together to settle it. There is no leader. In general, pygmies are peaceful people.

Pgymy men working in their village.

37

What do pygmies' houses look like?

To build a house, pygmies bend light, wooden poles together into a dome. The poles are covered with large leaves which also are used to make beds. Smaller leaves are used as dishes and cups.

What are pygmies' clothes like?

Clothing is made from the bark of the bongi tree. The bark is beaten and stretched before it is made into clothing. Because the weather is very hot, pygmies don't wear much at all.

Do pygmy children go to school?

Pygmy children don't attend school. Instead, their parents teach them how to hunt and gather food.

THE PEOPLE OF THE SAHARA

What is the world's largest desert?

The Sahara (suh-HAR-uh), in northern Africa, is the largest desert in the world. It is about the same size as the United States.

Sahara means both "desert" and "wilderness" in Arabic, the language of some of the Saharan people. A wilderness is a land that people have not yet changed or used. The modern Sahara has some towns, highways, factories, mines, and oil fields, but most of it is still a wilderness. Living there is very hard.

Some parts of the Sahara are sandy. Others are rocky, but all parts are hot and sunny during the day and cool at night.

Is all of the Sahara covered with sand?

No. Most of the Sahara Desert does *not* have
sand on it! In some areas, tiny pebbles called
gravel cover the ground. The middle of
the Sahara has the most sand.

A pile of sand formed by the wind is
called a sand dune. A few sand
dunes in the Sahara are as
high as the tallest buildings
in the world!

Who lives in the Sahara Desert?

There are three groups of people who live in the Sahara. The Moors live in the west. The Tuareg (TWAH-reg) live in the central part. The Tibbu (TIH-boo) live in the east. Each of these groups speaks a different language and has its own customs. Because they all live in the desert, however, their way of life is similar.

AFRICAN NOMAD

Thousands of years ago, the Sahara wasn't a desert. Old drawings in Saharan caves show people in canoes!

WHY DID I THINK THIS WOULD WORK?

How do desert people get water?

Even a desert has underground water in some places. Such a place is called an oasis (oh-AY-sis). At an oasis, the water may rise to the surface and form a spring or water hole. If it doesn't, people can dig a well to reach the water. In the Sahara, there are 90 big oases.

Before desert people leave an oasis, they fill goatskin bags with water. In this way, they have a supply of water while they travel.

How do desert people get food?

Some people live at an oasis and grow crops for food. They use ditches or pipes to run water from a well or spring to the crops. This system is called irrigation (ihr-ih-GAY-shun). Other desert people travel from one spot in the desert to another. These people are called nomads. They raise herds of animals and buy fruits and vegetables whenever they pass through a town.

Desert people can buy vegetables and grain from shops like this one when they pass through towns.

Why do nomads travel from one spot to another?

Most nomads keep traveling to find food and water for their herds of camels, sheep, or goats. Animals quickly eat the few plants that grow in the desert. Then the nomads have to find a new desert pasture, which is sometimes miles and miles away. When they get to a new pasture, they unpack and set up camp, but soon they will move again.

How do nomads carry all their supplies?

Supplies are carried on the backs of their camels. Camels can carry heavy loads. They are great helpers to desert nomads. Camels' soft, wide feet don't sink deeply into sand, so they can walk easily in the desert. Camels can also go without drinking water for a long time—seven to ten days when traveling. When there is little food, a camel can live on the fat stored in its hump.

Because camels are good at carrying supplies, some desert people use them to make a living. The camels carry supplies across the desert to be sold. People who sell things are called merchants. Desert merchants often travel together in groups called caravans (CARE-uh-vanz). A caravan can protect its members against robbers better than a few people traveling alone.

In the winter, a camel that does not work or travel can go without water for as long as two months!

How else do camels help desert people?

Camels not only *carry* supplies, but they *are* supplies themselves! Nomads drink camel milk and eat camel meat. From camel skins, nomads make leather for tents. From camel hair, they make wool clothes. Camels can also carry tired desert travelers on their backs.

What do nomads' houses look like?

Most nomads live in tents made of camel skins held up with poles. At moving time, the nomads fold up their tents and load them onto camels. Because nomads are moving all the time, they don't use the same kind of furniture that we do. They use mats woven from palm branches. Nomads use the mats for chairs, tables, and beds.

From years of walking on hot sand, the soles of nomads' feet are tough. Some can put their feet in a low fire and not feel it!

Do nomad children go to school?

Some do, but most nomad children do not attend a school like the one you go to. However, the governments of a few Saharan countries send teachers to nomads' camps so that children can get some schooling.

An Arabian family dines on a midday meal of rice.

What do nomads eat?

When desert families have guests, they often serve sheep or lamb that has been roasted over an open fire. On ordinary days, a desert cook boils the meat of a sheep, a lamb, or a chicken. Chick-peas and cut-up vegetables such as carrots, onions, and beans go into the same pot. A desert family also eats a dish called *couscous* (KOOS-koos), a cereal mixed with meat and vegetables.

Camel cheese and camel butter are also popular foods. Camel cheese is made from camel milk. Camel butter isn't. Camel butter is the fat taken from the camel's hump after the animal is killed. People spread it on certain foods, or just dip their fingers in it and eat it plain. Desert people drink sweet tea, goat milk, or camel milk.

43

Now let's sail across the Atlantic Ocean from Africa to South America. South America has modern cities, but much of it is covered by one of the world's great natural wonders—a huge rain forest!

THE WONDERS OF SOUTH AMERICA

THE COUNTRIES OF SOUTH AMERICA

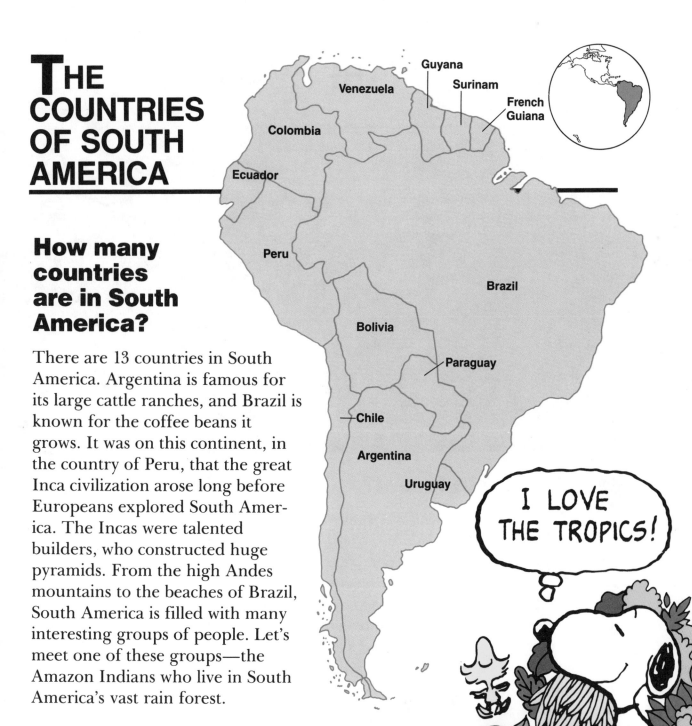

How many countries are in South America?

There are 13 countries in South America. Argentina is famous for its large cattle ranches, and Brazil is known for the coffee beans it grows. It was on this continent, in the country of Peru, that the great Inca civilization arose long before Europeans explored South America. The Incas were talented builders, who constructed huge pyramids. From the high Andes mountains to the beaches of Brazil, South America is filled with many interesting groups of people. Let's meet one of these groups—the Amazon Indians who live in South America's vast rain forest.

What is the largest country in South America?

Brazil is the largest. It takes up about half the continent. Some Brazilians live in modern cities. Others belong to tribes that live in the rain forest.

I LOVE THE TROPICS!

THE PEOPLE OF THE AMAZON RAIN FOREST

In the morning, a mist hangs over the Amazon's tropical rain forest. The words *tropic* and *tropical* are often used to refer to the hot regions around the equator.

What is a rain forest?

A rain forest is a very warm, very rainy place where many trees grow. Because of the rain, the trees grow tall and close together. The covering of treetops is so thick that it blocks out the wind, making the air below still and uncomfortable. The treetops also keep sunlight from reaching the ground. Because most plants need sunlight to live, few low plants can grow in much of the rain forest. It is quite easy to walk through these shaded areas that have few low plants. A rain forest has many different kinds of animals. These include birds, crocodiles, anteaters, lizards, snakes, and big cats called jaguars. The list also includes thousands of different kinds of insects, some of which are harmful or just bothersome to people.

The largest rain forest in the world is in South America, around the Amazon River. Most of the rain forest is in Brazil, but parts are in eight other countries. This rain forest is 3,000 miles long!

Is the rain forest the same as a jungle?

No. A jungle is a part— the thickest part—of a rain forest. It usually grows in places where people have chopped down the tall trees. After the area has been cleared, many ground plants grow quickly. In fact, plants grow on and over and around each other. This makes a jungle a very hard place to walk through.

How much rain falls in the Amazon rain forest?

A lot! In the wettest places, about 100 inches of rain falls in a year. That is more than twice the rainfall of New York City each year, and six times the yearly rainfall in Los Angeles.

In the rain forest, the wettest months are called the rainy season. Then heavy rain falls during part of every day. The rest of the year is the dry season, but even that is not very dry. It's just less wet!

There is always rain falling somewhere in the Amazon rain forest!

Who lives in the Amazon rain forest?

Groups of people we call Indians live there. These people are distantly related to the Indians of North America, but they look very different. They have darker skin and shorter bodies than North American Indians. Because they live in a rain forest, their way of life is very different, and their languages are different, too.

Until recently, the Amazon Indians lived exactly as their ancestors had lived thousands of years ago. The dense, rain forest kept them separated from the rest of the world, but today, life for the Amazon Indians is changing.

This Amazon father and son are natives of the rain forest.

What kind of houses do Amazon Indians build?

Some Amazon Indians build houses that look like haystacks. The houses are made of dried palm leaves or dried grasses. A frame of thin poles holds the "hay" in place.

Other Amazon Indians use the dried palm leaves only for roofs. They make the walls of their houses from either thin tree trunks or mud.

AMAZON HOUSES

How do these houses look inside?

Each house has one very big room. The floor is a natural dirt floor. The room has some stools made from tree trunks. It has hammocks to sleep in. There are no windows, so the house is dark. Sometimes the Amazon Indians build a fire inside to cook their food, but most of the time, they cook outdoors.

In many Amazon houses, parents, children, grandparents, aunts, and uncles all live together. Sometimes as many as 70 people live in one house!

What do rain forest people eat?

They eat many kinds of fruits and vegetables. They grow some in their gardens and gather some in the forest. They also hunt and fish for food.

Corn and cassava (kuh-SAH-vuh) are the most important crops in the Amazon rain forest. Cassava is the plant from which we make tapioca pudding. The Amazon Indians make cakes from it. They roast corn and make a soup of ground corn. They also raise and eat sweet potatoes.

Trees in the forest supply the native people with fruits and nuts, and bees provide them with honey. Some Amazon Indian groups are always on the lookout for a tree with a beehive in it. When they see one, they chop the tree down, take the honey from the hive, and eat it.

Amazon Indians also eat wild pigs, monkeys, armadillos (are-muh-DILL-oze), turtles, and fish. They roast the meat and fish over an open fire.

Amazon waters contain vicious piranha (pih-RAHN-yuh) fish. One piranha can fit in your hand. A group of piranhas could eat you up in just a few minutes!

NO SWIMMING

Do the Amazon Indians hunt with guns?

Yes. Sometimes they use shotguns to hunt large ground animals. For hunting birds, fish, and other small animals, however, they rely on their old ways—spears, blowguns, or bows and arrows.

Amazon Indians are very skilled hunters who can hit fast-moving animals with their arrows and darts. They can even hit fish with their arrows!

Rain forest hunters use bamboo stems to make long arrows and thin strips of palm wood to make bow strings. Some bows are as long as six feet, longer than the height of some hunters!

A blowgun is a long, hollow bamboo pole. Through it, a hunter blows poison darts.

Amazon people use river boats to travel through the rain forest.

Some of the Amazon Indians hunt at night with the help of flashlights!

Is it true that Amazon Indians wear no clothing?

Many Amazon Indians of the rain forest wear little or no clothing. Some wear only belts, arm bands, jewelry, or headbands. Some wear only tiny skirts called loincloths.

For special occasions, these rain forest natives paint their bodies with different colored dyes made from jungle plants. Some of the designs they use stand for animals in the rain forest.

Is it true that Amazon Indians of the rain forest are unfriendly?

Some of them dislike strangers. In the past, explorers hurt and killed many of them, and some were forced to work as slaves by people who came to take rubber from the forest's rubber trees.

Other Amazon Indians are shy rather than unfriendly. They are frightened by visitors, who are very different from themselves. Often, though, these native people learn to accept visitors as friends.

50

Who teaches the rain forest children?

Children are taught mostly by parents, friends, relatives, and older children, but they don't learn reading, writing, and arithmetic. Instead, children learn the skills they will need when they grow up. Girls learn how to cook, plant crops, and search for honey and fruit. They also practice weaving cloth. Boys learn to hunt and fish.

There are a few modern schools in the Amazon rain forest today. They were set up by the government of Brazil. In these schools, children read books and take tests—just as you do.

Do Amazon children have time for toys?

Yes, they do, but they have to make their own. Sometimes their parents help them. They use cornstalks, bits of wood, bones—whatever they can find—to make dolls, toy animals, and balls to play with.

In an Amazon Indian relay race, each man who runs carries a 100-pound log on his shoulders!

THIS ISN'T EASY!

What happens when people get sick in the rain forest?

Many Amazon Indians believe that evil spirits cause illness. When someone gets sick, a shaman is called. The shaman tries to cure the person by dealing with the spirits and by using natural medicines. Jungle villages do not have modern doctors and nurses. However, Brazilian doctors and nurses sometimes visit the rain forest to take care of sick people. There are now some Amazon Indian nurses and medical teams.

CHAPTER 7

From bustling cities to busy farming towns to quiet fishing villages—North America has something for everyone. It also has a place that might be fun to visit, if you don't mind frosty weather. Come follow Snoopy for a snow-crunching trip to the land of the Eskimos (ES-kuh-moze).

NEXT STOP: NORTH AMERICA

THE COUNTRIES OF NORTH AMERICA

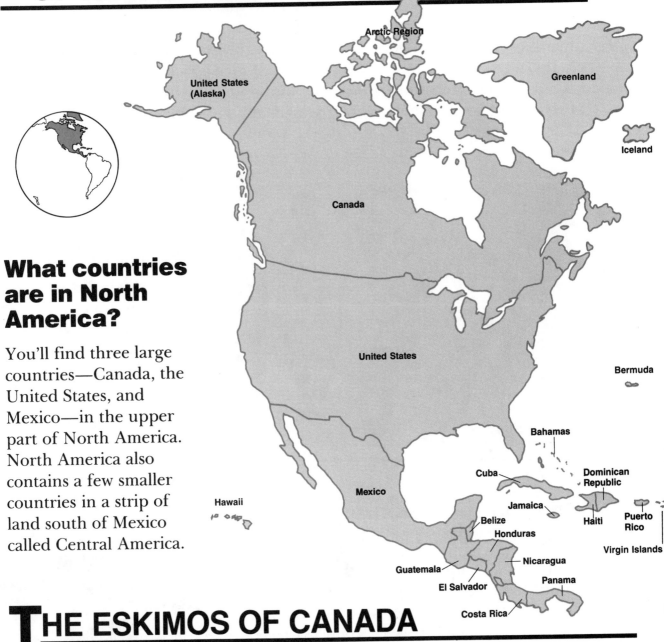

What countries are in North America?

You'll find three large countries—Canada, the United States, and Mexico—in the upper part of North America. North America also contains a few smaller countries in a strip of land south of Mexico called Central America.

THE ESKIMOS OF CANADA

Who lives in the coldest parts of North America?

Eskimos—or Inuits—do. Inuit is the name that most Eskimos call themselves. They live in northern Canada, Alaska, and Greenland. These cold regions near the North Pole are called arctic (ARK-tick) regions. There are only about 50,000 Eskimos in the world.

Do the Eskimos ever have warm weather?

Yes. The northern part of North America gets warm in the summer, but never hot. The average summer temperature there is about 50 degrees Fahrenheit. The summer temperature often drops below freezing, and sometimes it even snows! Although the ground isn't always covered with snow, it is always frozen below the surface. This frozen area is called permafrost.

Only strong plants can grow during the short, cool arctic summer. In spite of this, there are several kinds of arctic plants.

Eskimos wear warm clothing that is often quite colorful.

Do Eskimos live in igloos?

Although most modern Eskimos live in houses, some still live in igloos. These Eskimos move into tents in the summer months. Even though most Eskimos don't live in igloos, they still know how to build them from snow blocks. In igloos, even the beds are made out of snow blocks!

What do the Eskimos wear to keep warm?

Eskimos bundle up in warm clothes that are made out of fur, and they sleep under fur blankets. When it is very cold, Eskimos put on two layers of everything. The first layer of fur goes against their skin. In the second layer, the fur is worn on the outside. Eskimos also wear fur boots called *mukluks* (MUCK-lucks). The outer soles are made from the skin of a moose or seal, and the tops are made from canvas or caribou (KAR-uh-boo) skin. A caribou is a kind of deer that lives in the arctic.

HOW TO BUILD AN IGLOO BY SEYMOUR SNOW

Teams of dogs pull Eskimo sleds across the snow.

How do Eskimos travel over the snow?

At one time, Eskimos traveled in sleds pulled by dogs. Some Eskimos still travel this way, but most now use snowmobiles. For long distances, they use airplanes that have skis on them to help the planes land on ice.

For travel on water, Eskimos use motorboats, kayaks, and umiaks (OO-me-aks). Kayaks and umiaks are made of animal skins stretched over a wooden frame.

What games do Eskimos play?

Eskimos do a lot of playing indoors where it is warm. One of the games they play is like darts. The Eskimos make holes in a pair of antlers, hang them from the ceiling, and then try to throw sticks through the holes.

In spite of the cold weather, Eskimos still do play outdoors. Naturally, they play in the snow or on ice. Eskimo children like to speed downhill on sleds. They also enjoy other cold weather sports such as ice hockey and ice skating.

Are there schools for Eskimo children?

There are schools, but only in large villages. Children who live in small villages must leave their families to get an education. When they are ready to start first grade, they move to a village that has a school. Children from a few villages live together in a large building. Usually there are fewer than 30 children. At the end of the school year, the children go home.

DID YOU KNOW...?

SIBERIA, HERE I COME!

snowy part of Russia is in Asia. It is called Siberia and not many people live there. Some of the Slavic states, like Rumania, Latvia, and Croatia, are in Eastern Europe. Greece and Turkey are also on two continents.

• Russia and the independent Slavic states are on two continents—Asia and Europe. The

GREAT WALL OF CHINA

• The Great Wall of China lives up to its name! This amazing wall is 2,150 miles long, with many more miles of branches. In some sections, the wall rises to 39 feet above the ground! Built of earth and stone, it is 32 feet thick. The Great Wall was built by a Chinese emperor. He wanted to stop Mongolian horsemen from invading his country, but the plan didn't work. The invaders broke through the wall.

THAT'S A GREAT WALL YOU'RE BUILDING, LINUS!

● Have you ever traded marbles or baseball cards? If you have, you've used a system called bartering. All sorts of things have been bartered in the past—beads, shells, animal skins, feathers, and food. Today, most countries use money printed by their governments. Money has pictures and symbols that have meaning for the people who live in that country. Some people still don't use money. They barter for things they need. They might barter—trade—a chicken for a piece of cloth or a bushel of apples or an ax.

● Mexico City is sinking! The capital city of Mexico was built on a plateau on top of water. This water is pumped out of the soil and used for drinking water. As the water level in the soil gets lower, the soil gets lower, too. This means that the streets and buildings on top of the soil sink. Since 1900, parts of Mexico City have sunk as much as 25 feet!

● Most Eskimo dogs, called huskies, stay outside all the time, even in the coldest weather. They have very thick fur. To keep warm while they sleep, they spin around and around until they have made a hole in the snow. Then they snuggle down into the hole, which protects them from the wind.

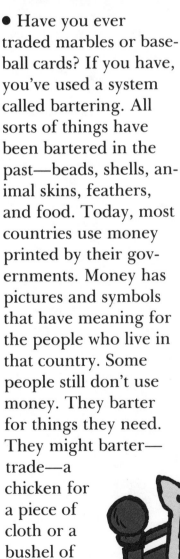

I'D RATHER USE A NICE BLANKET TO KEEP WARM!

People wear clothes for many different reasons. Charlie Brown wears a sweater to keep warm. Sally wears a dress with a bow because it makes her look pretty. Spike wears a hat to protect his head from the hot sun. Have you ever wondered how the first clothes were made? Let's find out!

A STITCH IN TIME

CHAPTER 8

CLOTH, THREAD, AND NEEDLES

Who invented cloth?

No one knows. We do know that 5,000 years ago, Africans were already making cloth from tree bark. Before Columbus discovered America, Native Americans were also making bark cloth. It is possible that other people may have made cloth before either of these groups did.

To make bark cloth, both the Africans and the Native Americans used the same method. First they crisscrossed wet pieces of bark. Then they pounded the bark with rocks. The tiny fibers that made up the bark stuck together. They formed a piece of cloth. Some Africans still make bark cloth this way.

A spider has special glands that make thread for webs.

Who invented thread?

Thread is made naturally by worms, insects, and spiders. A spider, for instance, has special glands that make thread that the spider uses to spin webs. The thread is released through tiny organs in the back of its body called spinnerets.

The first human thread makers probably got the idea for spinning thread from spiders. First, though, the human thread makers needed fibers to make their thread.

What fibers are good for thread?

Fibers from any tall, stringy plant can be used to make thread. You can make thread yourself from tall grasses or cattails. Hang the plants in a cool, dry place for two or three weeks. They will become very dry. Then carefully pull apart the fibers and braid or twist them into thread. Flax, hemp, and cotton are three plants grown for their fibers. We make linen from flax fibers, rope from hemp fibers, and cotton cloth from cotton fibers.

The hair from these llamas can be used to make thread.

Could you make thread from your dog's hair?

You could if you had enough of it, but you'd need a lot of hair to make a piece of cloth. If your dog is shedding, you might sweep up the hairs and try it. However, your dog would be *very unhappy* if you tried to get some of its hair in any other way!

What animal fibers can be used for thread?

Thread can be made from the hair of any animal. People in ancient Asia used the hair of sheep, camels, and goats. Early South Americans used wool from wild mountain animals, such as llamas (LAH-muz), vicuñas (vye-KOO-nyuhz), and alpacas. These three goatlike animals still live in the Andes Mountains of South America.

Native Americans of North America used horsehair, buffalo fur, and moose hair for thread making.

I DARE ANYONE TO TRY TO MAKE THREAD OUT OF ME!

What is spinning?

Spinning is a way of twisting many fibers together into one long thread. For hundreds of years, people used a spinning wheel to make thread. It could spin only one thread at a time. Today modern factories use huge machines to spin hundreds of threads at a time. Here's how a thread is made.

The fibers are placed in a straight line. The end of each fiber overlaps the beginning of the next fiber. When the fibers are twisted, they cling together. The more the fibers overlap, the stronger the thread. Extra fibers can be twisted in to make the thread thicker.

Who discovered how to make cloth from thread?

Probably fishermen in Egypt, 5,000 years ago, made the discovery. They made fish nets by knotting and tying threads. Nets were probably the first "cloth" made from thread.

Where did people get needles for sewing?

Before metal was discovered, prehistoric people carved needles from wood and bone. People who lived near the sea used fish bones and bits of shell. People in deserts used cactus spines.

Europeans were using metal needles about 2,500 years ago. Most Native Americans did not have metal tools before European settlers came to America just a few hundred years ago.

Prehistoric people carved needles from wood.

WEAVING

Who invented weaving?

We don't really know. Weaving is a special way of putting together threads to make cloth. The process may have been discovered by net makers. Net makers tied the ends of their threads around weights. The weights kept the threads from getting tangled. The weights also made the threads hang tight and straight while the net makers were working. The idea for a loom may have occurred to someone who was watching fishermen make their nets.

A loom is used to weave some fabrics.

What is a loom?

A loom is a machine for weaving. The loom keeps a whole row of threads tight and straight. This thread, or yarn, is called the warp. Another row of threads can then pass under and over the straightened threads. This thread is called filling yarn in the U.S. and weft yarn in England.

63

Snoopy never has to worry about what to wear. He always has a warm outfit! People throughout the ages, though, have always had different ideas about what kind of clothes to wear. So let's go along with Snoopy and see how clothing styles have changed over the years.

CLOTHES OF YESTERDAY, TODAY, AND TOMORROW

THE FIRST CLOTHES

What did the first clothes look like?

They were pieces of cloth or fur. People wrapped them around their waists, the way you wrap yourself in a towel. You've probably seen pictures of cave dwellers dressed this way. To keep warm, people wrapped other pieces of fur or cloth over their shoulders. Another early form of clothing was the tunic (TOO-nik). People in Central Asia were wearing tunics 5,000 years ago.

What is a tunic?

A tunic is a long shirt made of two pieces of fur or cloth. One piece is for the front, and one is for the back. The pieces are sewn together at the shoulders and at the sides. Tunics can be long or short. In ancient Greece, more than 2,500 years ago, men wore tunics just above their knees. Women's tunics reached to the ground.

Did the ancient Greeks wear underwear?

A poor person in ancient Greece had only one tunic—which was both underwear and outerwear. A richer person wore a tunic as underwear, and a *himation* (hih-MAT-ee-on), or toga, over the tunic.

What is a toga?

A toga is a large piece of cloth worn over one or both shoulders. Togas were popular for many years in ancient Greece and Rome. An ordinary man's toga was smaller than a rich man's toga. A rich man wore his toga draped around his body several times. An ordinary man draped his only once. Togalike clothing is a style today in some parts of the world, especially Africa.

In ancient Greece and Rome, men and women wore togas.

Most ancient Greeks went barefoot, even in the street!

In what other way did clothes show a person's wealth?

In ancient Rome, colors were the best way to know how wealthy a person was. Peasants were allowed to wear only one color, and usually it was brown or gray. The higher a person's rank was, the more colors he or she was allowed to wear. Colors also showed what a person did for a living.

How did colors show a person's job?

In ancient Rome, many jobs required clothing of certain colors. Here is a list of some of them.

purple, gold	royalty
purple stripe	high court official
blue	philosopher
black	religious leader
green	medical man

Some rich Roman women would wear several different colored tunics on top of each other. They would fold them so that all the different colors showed!

PANTS FOR MEN

When did men start wearing pants?

The first pants we know about were worn 2,500 years ago in Persia (now called Iran). Both men and women in ancient Persia wore pants.

The Persians traded with people from Central Asia. The Central Asians were nomads, people without settled homes, who lived in tents and moved from camp to camp. These nomads also wore pants. Today no one is sure if the Persians copied the style from the nomads or if the nomads copied the style of the Persians!

What did men in other parts of the world wear before they wore pants?

After they wore tunics, men in Europe wore stockings and pantaloons. Pantaloons were wide, loose, short pants. The men also wore high boots and capes or long jackets.

This drawing shows a European man wearing pantaloons.

Men in the 1600s wore high-heeled shoes and silk stockings trimmed with bows and lace!

When did long pants come into fashion for men?

Around 1800. Before that time, long pants were worn only by common workingmen. Rich men wore knee-length pants over stockings.

In 1789 a revolution began in France. The common people overthrew their rich rulers. After that, no one wanted to look rich. All men began wearing long pants.

JACKETS, TIES, RAINCOATS, AND ZOOT SUITS

When did men start wearing jackets?

The modern jacket came into use in England on December 15, 1660. Before then, Englishmen wore short capes. They copied the style from the French and bought many capes made in France.

King Charles II of England wanted his people to stop buying clothes from France. So on December 15, 1660, he appeared in court dressed in a Turkish-style jacket. He knew that everyone would copy his style and give up French capes.

The King of France was angry at Charles's fashion change. To get even, he made all the servants in the French court wear jackets.

Why were ties invented?

Ties were first meant to be like bibs. If a man dropped a piece of food, it would most likely hit his tie. The tie was easier to clean than a shirt. Eventually, men's ties became a good way to add decoration to a plain suit.

Who invented raincoats?

Raincoats were probably invented by soldiers, shepherds, and other people who had to spend a lot of time outside in bad weather.

Cloaks were the first rainwear. A cloak was just a flat piece of leather or heavy cloth. Its owner might have rubbed animal fat into the leather to make it waterproof. When rain began to come down, he simply threw the cloak over his head.

What are some unusual styles men have worn?

At various times, men have worn huge capes, very long feathers in hats, and tight starched collars. One unusual men's style of modern times was the zoot suit. It was popular with some American men in the 1930s and 1940s. The style called for a baggy jacket that reached to the knees and baggy pants that came up to the chest. The suit was usually dark-colored with thin light stripes. With it, men sometimes wore a long chain that hung from the chest nearly to the floor. The men usually put on suspenders to hold up the pants, and topped off their outfits with floppy hats.

ZOOT SUIT

WOMEN'S HOOP SKIRTS, CORSETS, PANTS, AND PANTYHOSE

What was a hoop skirt?

A hoop skirt was a petticoat that looked like a cage. A woman wore a hoop under a dress or skirt. The skirt covered the "cage." The hoop skirt held the skirt out much as a metal frame supports a lampshade. Some hoop skirts folded up when women sat down.

When the style of huge skirts first became popular, women made their skirts stand out by wearing many petticoats at once. All those petticoats made it hard for women to get around because their clothes weighed too much. In the 1700s, women started wearing hoop skirts to lessen the weight.

What is an hourglass figure?

From the 1840s until the early 1900s, people thought that a beautiful woman should have the shape of an hourglass. This meant that she had to be very small in the middle and wide above and below that. To help give themselves an hourglass shape, women wore either very full skirts or bustles. A bustle was a puff of cloth at the back of a skirt, often held up by a wire hoop. The hoop collapsed when the woman sat down. Women's waists were pulled in very tightly with underwear belts called corsets.

A girl began tightening her waist when she was about 14. Every morning she put on her corset—even if she was playing tennis that day! As the girl grew older, her corset was laced tighter and tighter. It kept her waistline from growing. A few women's waists were only 18 inches around! Most modern women have waists at least six inches larger than that.

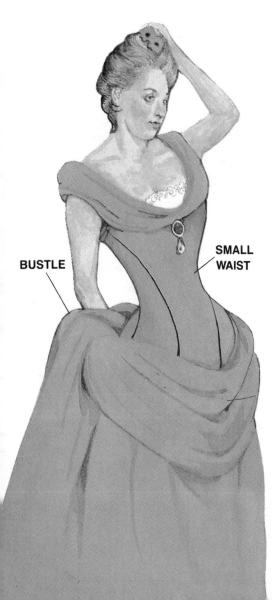

BUSTLE

SMALL WAIST

In the 1800s, women wore corsets under their dresses to give them small waists, and bustles to help give them hourglass figures.

Amelia Bloomer

Wasn't it hard for women to breathe in tight corsets?

It certainly was. Corsets were both uncomfortable and unhealthy. That is why women began to talk about wearing more comfortable clothes. In 1850, Amelia Bloomer tried to get women to wear shorter dresses with roomy trousers—without corsets. People laughed at her idea and called her trousers bloomers, but Mrs. Bloomer won in the long run. About 50 years later, women got tired of being unable to move around. They started to wear simpler, looser clothes.

YIKES!

LET'S FACE IT, MARCIE. I JUST DON'T THINK CORSETS ARE FOR ME!

When did women start wearing pants?

In many countries of the world, pants have been part of women's clothing for hundreds of years. In Europe and the United States, pants for women were not considered proper until the 1920s. Movie stars helped make pants popular in America. The stars wore loose pajamas of shiny materials for lounging at home or at the beach. By the 1930s, women were wearing pants for sports and to parties as well.

While we were fighting World War II—from 1941 to 1945—many women worked in factories. They replaced men who had gone to war. The women factory workers wore overalls and other men's clothes. By the time the war ended, women were used to the comfort of pants, and began wearing pants more and more often.

Women wore "slacks" while working in factories during World War II.

During World War II, there wasn't enough silk for stockings. To make it look as though they were wearing stockings, women painted lines to look like seams on the back of their legs!

When were pantyhose invented?

Pantyhose became popular in the 1960s when miniskirts, very short skirts, became popular. Before then, women wore stockings that were held up by belts, called garter belts. These belts had hooks that fastened onto the stockings. Made of silk or nylon, the stockings were like long socks that came up to the thigh.

CHANGING STYLES

Why do styles change?

Styles are set by the people who design, make, and sell clothes. Ordinary people would not buy new clothes as often as they do if styles did not change.

Certain styles come and go very quickly. These styles are called fads. Fads sometimes are started in different parts of the country. For example, in California, where the weather is warm, people began to wear colorful boxer shorts which soon became popular all over the country. Rock stars, rap singers, and movie stars can also start fads. Lots of people will copy a style after they see it on someone famous.

How have women's styles changed?

The lengths of skirts and dresses are always changing. In the 1950s, women and girls wore big skirts that hung below their knees. Circle skirts decorated with poodle appliqués were called poodle skirts. Styles became more daring in the 1960s, when miniskirts were popular. For a while, very long skirts, called maxiskirts, became popular, but when it rained, the bottom of the skirt would get wet! Women wanted skirts that weren't so long.

Today skirt lengths change from short to longer and back again almost every year. Women and girls can choose to wear just about any length, depending on what they find comfortable. Many women who have to dress up for work wear business suits with matching jackets and skirts.

In what other ways have styles changed?

In the last 50 years, many clothes seem to have gone back and forth between expanding and shrinking, without even being washed! Men's ties, jacket lapels, and pant legs have become wider and narrower, depending on the current style. In the early 1970s, some ties were so wide that they actually looked like bibs! Pant legs, too, went from being very narrow at the ankle to being very wide and floppy. These wide pants were called bell-bottoms. Today pant legs have shrunk back to a medium size.

Elephant bells are not something you use to call an elephant to dinner! They were pants that had such wide, flared bottoms that they looked like ringing bells as the wearer walked!

What will clothes look like in the future?

We don't know exactly what styles people will wear. Fashion changes in strange ways, but in the future we may wear fewer clothes. We probably won't need heavy winter coats because scientists in the space program have invented new types of cloth. One type is a warm, lightweight cloth used for astronauts' clothes. Some raincoats and other clothes are made of sturdy, lightweight cloth invented by space program scientists.

Today, more clothes, like jeans, T-shirts, sweatpants, and vests, are unisex and both boys and girls can wear them.

CHAPTER 10

Cowboys, Native Americans, and the settlers who moved west across the United States played a major role in how we dress today. Moccasins, vests, and cowboy hats are just a few of their contributions. So saddle up your horse with Sheriff Spike. He'll tell you all about Western clothes.

WESTERN DUDS

NATIVE AMERICANS

What did the Native Americans wear?

Before the settlers came to America, many Native Americans wore leather tunics. In cold weather, they put on leggings—pieces of fur or leather which they wrapped around their legs. The leggings came up over their knees like long socks. Native Americans also wore soft leather shoes called moccasins.

Native Americans and early settlers sometimes kept their feet warm in winter by stuffing grass into the toes of their moccasins!

SURE BEATS COLD FEET!

How did Native American styles change after the settlers came?

After meeting European women, Native American women in the Northeast began wearing skirts and blouses. The fashion of cloth shirts spread among Native American men. In the Southwest, Native American lands were settled by people from Spain. Spanish men wore long pants made of cloth. Soon the Native Americans started to wear cloth pants, too.

How did Native Americans decorate their clothes?

Glass beads were a favorite Native American decoration. Native Americans would trade furs and blankets with the settlers for the brightly colored beads. They sewed the beads onto their tunics and moccasins and weaved them into their belts. Native American men also wore locks of hair on their shirts.

Colorful clothes and headgear were worn by Native Americans.

Did that hair come from people who were scalped?

Sometimes, but usually the men cut off some of their own hair or their wives' hair. Sometimes a Native American gave some hair to a friend who had saved his life.

What did Native Americans wear in battle?

Some fought in armor, a hard covering that protects a person in battle. The northwestern Native Americans made chest armor from thin strips of wood and leather. Around a warrior's neck was a wooden collar. It covered his chin and mouth, too. On his head he wore a carved wooden helmet. The helmet took the form of either a fierce-looking person or an animal. The human face was supposed to scare the enemy. The animal face was supposed to bring the warrior good luck. The wood protected the man from clubs and arrows.

Other Native Americans fought bare-chested. They protected their chests with shields. A shield is a flat piece of armor that a warrior carries on his arm. Native American shields were often made of buffalo skins. The skins were dried to make them strong and hard.

Did their chiefs wear huge headdresses to war?

No. It would have been difficult for a chief actually to have worn a headdress in battle. He wouldn't have been able to keep the feathers out of his way. Headdresses were called war bonnets because many of the decorations and feathers were prizes given for deeds in war. The bonnets were worn only for special ceremonies.

COWBOY GEAR

Why did cowboys wear such big hats?

The big domes and wide brims of cowboy hats kept the sun, rain, and snow off the cowboys' faces. Weather, however, was not the only reason a cowboy wore a hat. Cowboys didn't have cups or glasses out on the range. When a cowboy found a stream, he often put water in his hat and drank from the hat. Sometimes cowboys would bring water back to their horses in their hats.

Why were cowboy hats called ten-gallon hats?

Some of the cowboy hats were so big that they looked as if they could carry ten gallons of water. Of course, they couldn't. A hat would have to be awfully big to hold ten gallons, but the name stuck anyway.

What else did old-time cowboys wear?

When cowboys were working, they dressed in shirts and heavy work pants. If it was very cold, they added another shirt, not a jacket. Jackets made it too hard for the cowboys to move their arms. Vests also helped keep them warm.

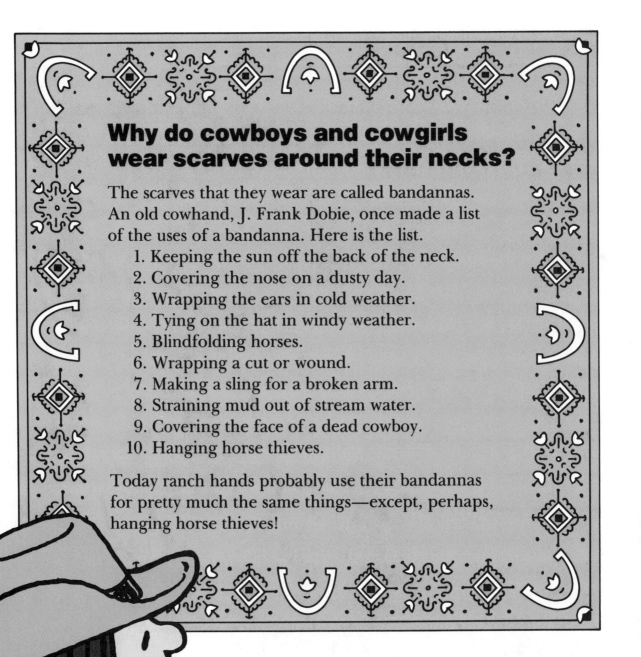

Why do cowboys and cowgirls wear scarves around their necks?

The scarves that they wear are called bandannas. An old cowhand, J. Frank Dobie, once made a list of the uses of a bandanna. Here is the list.

1. Keeping the sun off the back of the neck.
2. Covering the nose on a dusty day.
3. Wrapping the ears in cold weather.
4. Tying on the hat in windy weather.
5. Blindfolding horses.
6. Wrapping a cut or wound.
7. Making a sling for a broken arm.
8. Straining mud out of stream water.
9. Covering the face of a dead cowboy.
10. Hanging horse thieves.

Today ranch hands probably use their bandannas for pretty much the same things—except, perhaps, hanging horse thieves!

Why do cowboys and cowgirls wear high-heeled boots?

High heels keep the feet of horseback riders from slipping out of stirrups. This is very important. Riders can easily fall off their horses if their feet aren't in the stirrups.

Where did cowboy styles come from?

Cowboy styles came to North America from Spain. The Spanish settlers brought cattle with them. They also brought cattlemen. Spanish cattlemen wore wide leather hats called sombreros (some-BRE-rows). They also wore leather vests, leather boots with metal spurs, and leather chaps.

What are chaps?

Chaps are heavy leg coverings that are worn on the outside of jeans or pants. They are made of tough leather and protect the cowhand's legs from thorns and cold when he or she is out riding.

Do modern ranch workers wear chaps?

Yes. People still wear chaps, but not as much as they used to. These days, cowboys in North America ride more often in cars or trucks than on horses. In South America, many cowboys still ride horses to do their work, so they still need chaps.

RIDE'M, COWBOY!

PIONEER CLOTHES

What clothes were in style for men of the Old West?

Wealthy men in the Old West copied eastern styles. They wore suits with matching long pants and jackets. With the suits, they put on fancy silk or velvet vests. They also wore white shirts and bow ties, and tall black top hats.

Most of the other people in the Old West worked the land. Because of this, they wore tough, rugged clothes that wouldn't be ruined by hard work.

WILD BILL HICKOK

WILD SALLY BROWN

Did pioneers ever wear Native American clothes?

Some men did. Wild Bill Hickok, a famous frontier scout and marshal, was known for his fancy Native American clothes. He wore tunics of soft leather embroidered with beads. He carried silver guns with ivory handles.

When were blue jeans invented?

In the 1850s, Levi Strauss began making heavy brown pants for the gold miners in San Francisco. Strauss put copper rivets in all the places where pants usually rip. This made them extra strong. Soon he began dying the pants he made blue. He called them blue jeans.

Levi Strauss first went to California to look for gold, but he ended up making much more money from selling pants than from panning gold!

What did women in the Old West wear?

A pioneer woman or girl usually wore a blouse and a long cotton skirt. She often had an apron to cover it, and when she went out, she threw a shawl over her shoulders. Sometimes in cold weather, women wore leather leggings like those of Native American women.

What did pioneer women wear to dress up?

A pioneer woman or girl usually had one good dress for going to church and to parties. One popular style about 100 years ago was the very full skirt. Pioneer women also tried to keep up with the latest styles from back East, which included the newest fashions in bonnets and shawls.

LUCY, MAY I HELP YOU WITH YOUR SHAWL?

CHAPTER · 11

Shorts, T-shirts, sneakers, and sweat suits are clothes we wear for sports and other leisure activities. These clothes give a person lots of room to move, but some sports call for special outfits. Swimmers need bathing suits, baseball catchers need face masks, and scuba divers need flippers. Here are some of the special clothes that are needed for different sports.

ON YOUR MARK, GET SET, GO!

MASKS, GLOVES, PADS, AND HELMETS

Do people ever wear masks in everyday life?

Masks are worn for many sports. Skiers sometimes wear knitted wool masks to keep their faces warm and to protect them from frostbite. Scuba divers and snorkelers wear masks to help them see underwater. Hockey goalies wear masks to protect their faces from flying pucks. Baseball catchers wear masks, too.

Why do baseball catchers need masks?

Catchers wear masks to protect their faces. A ball comes in very fast from a pitcher. If a batter hits a foul ball, it can bounce into the catcher's face. The mask stops it. Masks also protect the catcher from a bat that swings out of control.

What other protection does a catcher wear?

A catcher has a chest pad and shin guards. These serve the same purpose as the mask—to protect the catcher from fast balls and flying bats. A catcher also has a special padded glove called a mitt, which protects the catcher's hand.

What do the other baseball gloves look like?

For all positions other than catcher, the gloves have fingers that are sewn together. There is webbing between the fingers and the thumb. The first baseman's glove is much larger than those worn by other players because first basemen have to scoop up many balls off the ground.

What clothes do football players wear for protection?

In football, players wear helmets and pads. The pads are worn on their shoulders, ribs, hips, thighs, and knees. The shoulder pads have steel springs. Sometimes the leg pads are sewn into the pants. The pads help to protect the football player who is hit or knocked down.

What does a football player's helmet look like?

The helmet, made of unbreakable plastic, is padded on the inside. There is a bar across the front of the helmet to protect the player's face. Helmets have chin straps to secure the helmet. Players also wear mouth guards to protect their lips and teeth.

Did football players always have this much protection?

No. In the early days of football, they didn't have pads or helmets at all. The players wore pants and sweaters. The pants were made from heavy canvas. It wasn't until many players got hurt that pads and helmets were added.

What clothes do hockey players wear for protection?

Like football players, hockey players must be well-protected. Players wear gloves, leg pads, shoulder and arm pads, and helmets. Hockey helmets look a little different from football helmets because they don't have bars in front.

The goalie, the player who guards the goal area, has to wear extra protection. Stopping a fast hockey puck can be a dangerous job. To protect themselves, goalies wear heavy leg pads, chest protectors, and helmets with face masks. They also wear a special pair of gloves. One has a stiff board on the back to block flying pucks, and the other is a heavy-duty catching glove.

HELMET AND FACE MASK

CHEST PROTECTOR

CATCHING GLOVE

STICK GLOVE

STICK

PADS

SKATES

GOALIE

ON THE ATHLETE'S FOOT

What type of shoes are worn for sports?

It seems as if each sport has its own special type of shoe. These shoes are designed to help the athletes play their sport better. Here are some of the different types of shoes for different sports.

Soccer—Soccer players wear shoes with cleats, or knobs, on the bottom. The knobs grip the ground, so the player doesn't slip.

Hockey—Hockey games are played on the ice, so hockey players must wear ice skates. Skates look like a high shoe with a thin metal blade attached to the bottom.

Scuba Diving—Scuba divers wear flippers. Made of plastic, flippers are large, wide, and flat, like a duck's foot. Flippers help divers move through the water fast.

Skiing—Skis don't just attach themselves to a skier's regular shoe. The skier needs a special boot. Ski boots are usually made of plastic with warm padding inside. The boots have a special place where they can attach to the skis.

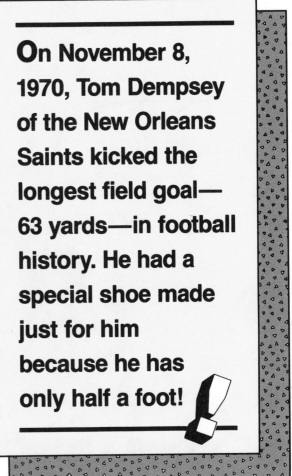

Swimming—Swimmers go barefoot!

Golf—Golfers must keep their feet planted firmly in one place when they swing. For this reason, they wear shoes with metal spikes on the bottom.

Runners—Too much running can be bad for a runner's bones if he or she doesn't have enough cushion for the feet. This is why runners' shoes have thick rubber soles. Runners' shoes also are light so the runner doesn't have to lift up too much weight with each step.

On November 8, 1970, Tom Dempsey of the New Orleans Saints kicked the longest field goal— 63 yards—in football history. He had a special shoe made just for him because he has only half a foot!

SUPER SWIM WEAR

How do bathing suits help swimmers?

When cloth absorbs water, it gets heavy. Heavy clothing can slow a swimmer down or even make the swimmer sink. Today's bathing suits don't have very much cloth, and they are made of fabric that doesn't absorb much water. This type of lightweight bathing suit came into use only in the past 50 years.

What did the old-time bathing suits look like?

In the 1850s and 1860s, women on the beach wore suits with long pants, full skirts, and high collars. On their feet, they wore canvas bathing slippers. When all that clothing got wet, it was very heavy.

Little by little, bathing suits got smaller. About 90 years later, the bikini was invented. That barely covered anything!

What did old-time bathing suits for men look like?

Most men didn't wear special suits for bathing until about the 1850s. At that time, men and women started going to the beach together. At first, men wore just bathing trunks. By the 1870s, however, people were becoming more modest, so men covered up with knitted tops that were like T-shirts. Their trunks reached to the tops of their knees. This style lasted for about 50 years.

Men wore bathing suits like these in the 1890s.

What is a wet suit?

A wet suit must be worn in very cold water. It is worn mostly by scuba divers and surfers. A wet suit covers the entire body. It is made of rubber with lots of bubbles in it. The bubbles help the diver float. Wet suits are skintight, but they allow a tiny bit of water to leak in. The wearer's body heat warms up the water very quickly. This thin layer of water then keeps the body warm.

CHAPTER 12

KEEPING THINGS UNIFORM

Look all around you. Everyone seems to be wearing something different, but sometimes people wear exactly the same thing. When police officers, fire fighters, or airline pilots get dressed to go to work, their clothes are exactly alike. That's because they're wearing uniforms. If you play team sports or are a member of a scout group, you probably have a uniform, too!

KNIGHTS IN ARMOR

What is armor?

Armor is any protection that a person wears into battle. Most people think that, long ago, armor was made of metal, but sometimes it was made of wood or leather.

WHY DO I LET HIM TALK ME INTO THESE THINGS?...

Metal chest armor and helmets helped protect early soldiers from enemy arrows.

When did soldiers start wearing metal armor?

About 3,500 years ago. At that time, soldiers in the Middle Eastern countries of Assyria (uh-SIHR-ee-uh) and Babylon (BAB-uh-lun) sewed pieces of metal to their leather tunics. The metal gave warriors protection against enemy arrows. About 2,500 years ago, the Greeks wore metal helmets, and large pieces of metal on their chest and backs.

Much later, about 600 years ago, soldiers in Europe, called knights, began to wear full suits of armor. A suit of armor covered a soldier's whole body. Made of large pieces of metal joined together, the armor had hinges at the knees and elbows. A metal helmet covered the soldier's face, head, and neck.

What kind of shoes did knights wear?

Knights wore metal even on their feet. These shoes were pointy like the rest of the shoes of that time. The metal shoes were usually carefully fitted to the knight's feet.

How did a knight move around in all that armor?

He couldn't move very easily! Young knights had to train themselves to carry the extra weight, but their horses had the worst part of the deal. Knights rode horses into battle because that was the only way they could move quickly, so the horses had to carry the knight with all his heavy armor. Sometimes even the horses wore armor!

English soldiers 400 years ago used suits of armor such as this.

A full suit of armor—from helmet to foot pieces—weighed 55 to 65 pounds!

What did ordinary soldiers wear?

Until 400 years ago, most common soldiers wore leather tunics and helmets. Sometimes the leather was covered with small pieces of metal. In some countries, common soldiers wore chain mail under their tunics. Chain mail is a cloth made of tiny metal chains linked together. It protected the wearer from spears and arrows. Since the soldiers' tunics had no sleeves, only chain mail covered their arms. Some knights wore chain mail, too, but they wore it under a metal chest plate.

In the 1500s in Europe, some people slashed up their clothes to be in style. They copied this fashion from soldiers who had been in battle!

SOLDIERS IN UNIFORM

What do modern soldiers wear?

Today soldiers wear uniforms made of cloth. Each uniform has a name tag and a rank on it. Some have medals and patches on them. The color of the uniform shows what country the soldier is fighting for. For instance, in the Civil War, the Union soldiers wore blue, and the Confederate soldiers wore gray. The color of a soldier's uniform was important because no one wanted to mistake a friend for an enemy.

Are all the uniforms of one country the same color?

No. The color and style of the uniforms change with the different branches of the military. The four major military branches in the United States are the army, navy, air force, and marines.

What is a camouflage uniform?

Camouflage clothes are colored green and brown and gray like the plants, trees, and dirt outside. Such clothes help soldiers hide from the enemy. When a soldier is wearing camouflage clothes, the soldier will blend into the trees and plants in a forest.

What do the decorations on the uniforms mean?

Stripes, bars, and stars tell a soldier's rank—how important he or she is in the armed services. A beginning soldier may have a patch with one stripe. A longtime soldier may have eight stripes. Officers have bars and stars. A four-star general is one of the most important officers in the army.

Medals and patches also show what the soldier has done. Soldiers get different kinds of medals for bravery, special skills, and good service.

96

EVERYDAY PEOPLE IN UNIFORM

Do children wear uniforms?

Yes. Scouts wear uniforms. In most countries, children wear uniforms to school. In the United States, children who go to public schools don't wear uniforms, but many children in private schools do.

Many Japanese school children wear uniforms.

Are there other kinds of uniforms?

Yes. Here are some pictures of different people wearing uniforms. Their special clothing shows what kind of work they do.

Railroad conductor

Nurses

Police officers

Chefs

What you wear sometimes depends on where in the world you live. In different cultures and climates, clothes may have special meanings or purposes. Let's join the *Peanuts* gang for a quick fashion trip around the world to see special clothes from head to toe.

CLOTHES AROUND THE WORLD

Hats, Crowns, and Wigs

Why do chefs wear tall white hats?

Chefs have been wearing white hats since at least 600 years ago. Back then, most Europeans wore special clothes to indicate their jobs. Bakers and cooks wore short, puffy white hats. Styles changed over the years, though, and in the 1900s, cooks started wearing tall white hats with puffs on the top. We now recognize the tall white hat as the sign of a restaurant chef.

Why do kings and queens wear crowns?

A crown sets a ruler apart from other people. A crown is a symbol that stands for power. Each crown has a design that represents its own country. When a country crowns its rulers, it gives them power over the country.

Kings and queens don't wear crowns all the time. Crowns are only for special ceremonies. Many crowns are heavy with gold and jewels. No person can wear one for very long without getting a headache.

Some of the clothes of King Henry VIII (the Eighth) of England had so many jewels sewn on them that no cloth showed through!

HOW DO I LOOK IN BEAGLE BLUE?

Why do lawyers and judges in England wear white wigs?

The English lawyer's wig is a style left over from 300 years ago. At that time, all important men in England wore wigs. The wigs had long curls that came down over the men's shoulders. When wig styles changed around the year 1700, lawyers and judges kept the older-style wigs as a sign of the importance of the law. In the 1790s, it was the style for men to put powder on their wigs. Some wigs were powdered white. Other wigs were light pink, silver, or blue!

Is it true that George Washington wore a wig?

No. People often say he did because wigs were in style for important men at the time of the American Revolution. Although many of the men who founded the United States wore wigs, Washington did not. He powdered his own hair and pulled it back in a ponytail.

Hair styles worn by rich women in the 1770s were almost three feet high!

Do people wear wigs today?

Yes. Sometimes actors wear wigs to look more like the characters they are playing. Other people wear wigs because they have lost their own hair. Modern wigs look very much like real hair. Wigs worn by men to cover bald spots are called toupees (too-PAYS).

VEILS, SANDALS, AND TURBANS

Why do women in some countries wear veils?

Veils are supposed to keep men from seeing women. This custom is very old. Women were wearing veils in a Middle Eastern country called Ur as far back as 5,000 years ago.

A few religions forbid women to show their faces. Some women who belong to the Muslim faith cover every part of their bodies except their eyes.

Do any men wear veils?

Yes. Among the Tuareg (TWAH-reg) people of the Sahara Desert, all men cover their faces. Women go without veils. Tuareg men believe that they are special, so ordinary people may not see their faces. Tuareg men wear veils even when they eat and drink!

Loose clothes help keep people cool in desert climates.

What else do people in the Sahara Desert wear?

Tuareg people wear sandals with big, wide soles shaped like paddles. The wide soles keep their feet from sinking into the sand.

They also wear what most desert people wear—loose clothes. Loose clothes allow air to reach a person's body easily. The air helps to keep the body cool. Some desert people dress in long, flowing robes. Others wear loose shirts and trousers.

Sahara Desert dwellers protect their heads from the sun by covering them with cloth or wrapping them in turbans.

What is a turban?

A turban is a long piece of cloth that is wound around a person's head. Men wear turbans in Egypt, India, Saudi Arabia, and other Asian and African countries. In some African countries, women wear turbans.

Wrapping a turban is like tying a huge knot, with your head at the center. You pass the ends of the turban over and under each other. Then you tuck the ends of the turban under the folds of cloth.

There are hundreds of different ways to wrap a turban. The way one is wrapped sometimes shows what tribe the wearer comes from.

Turbans are worn by many men in Asia and Africa.

Some Asian and African men wear modern shirts and pants, but still wear turbans!

DIRNDLS AND KILTS

What is a dirndl?

A dirndl is a brightly colored skirt that used to be worn by peasant women in Austria. Now makers of children's clothes have copied the style, and many girls' skirts and dresses are made in the dirndl style. The skirt is very full, and it is usually embroidered at the bottom. It is pulled in tight at the waist. A white apron is often draped over the front.

Do any men wear skirts?

In a few countries, men sometimes wear skirts. These styles have been worn in their countries for hundreds of years.

For special occasions, some Scottish men dress in knee-length skirts called kilts. Kilts are woven in brightly colored plaids. Each Scottish plaid belongs to a different family, or clan.

The guards at the Greek parliament building also wear kilts. The Greek kilts are white.

Kilts are part of traditional Scottish dress.

KIMONOS, SARONGS, MUUMUUS, AND SARIS

What is a kimono?

The kimono is the traditional dress of the Japanese people. It is a long robe with wide sleeves and a wide sash. It is usually decorated with many beautiful designs and colors. Both men and women wear kimonos, but these days, they are worn only on special occasions.

What is a sarong?

A sarong is a long piece of cloth that is wrapped around the body once. People who live on islands in the Pacific wear sarongs. So do people of Southeast Asia. Men wrap their sarongs at their waists. Women wrap theirs under their arms.

Some people in Africa wear clothes that look very much like sarongs.

What is a muumuu?

Some women in Hawaii wear long, loose cotton dresses called muumuus (MOO-mooz). The style began when settlers arrived in Hawaii in the 1800s. They thought the Hawaiian women weren't wearing enough, so they made them cover up with muumuus.

ALOHA, SWEETIE.

What is a sari?

A sari is a long piece of cloth worn by women in India and neighboring countries. It is usually made of silk or some other thin material. Before dressing in a sari, a woman puts on a short blouse and a half-slip. She tucks one end of the sari into the slip and wraps the other end around her body a few times and then puts it over her shoulder. The bottom of the sari reaches the floor.

A young Indian girl in a brightly-colored sari

GETAS AND BARE FEET

What do Eastern people wear on their feet?

In China, Japan, and other East Asian countries, people wear shoes like ours, but rope or straw sandals are also popular. One style of Japanese sandal is called a *geta* (GEH-tah). A *geta* has a thick wooden sole. In cold places, such as Tibet and Mongolia, people wear boots of fur or heavy cloth.

People who live on the Pacific Islands often go barefoot since the weather is warm.

What do African people wear on their feet?

What they wear on their feet depends on where they live and how much money they have. Jungle dwellers go barefoot. Others, too poor to buy shoes, also go barefoot. Some people can afford sandals. In African cities, many people wear Western-style shoes. Western-style means similar to clothing styles that come from modern Europe or America, parts of the world called the West.

Are there people who don't wear any clothes at all?

Only a very few of the world's people go naked. They live in isolated parts of Australia, South America, and Africa. They belong to tribes that have not met many people from other places. However, people who wear no clothes decorate their bodies with paint and dress up in colorful jewelry for special occasions.

About 300 years ago, some European women wore shoes with platforms up to 30 inches high!

DID YOU KNOW...?

GUESS WHO?

Behind the Mask

Lots of children wear masks when they go trick-or-treating on Halloween every year. Modern kids aren't the first people to wear masks, though. More than 10,000 years ago, cave dwellers in Europe wore masks. Before a hunt, they held special dances. They believed the dances would help them have a good hunt. At the dance, they wore masks of animals they were going to hunt.

Don't Sneeze in That Suit!

Because the space suits worn during early space flights were pressurized, astronauts could not touch their faces with their hands. This made it impossible to blow their noses! To scratch an itch, astronauts would have to rub the itchy part of their faces against the inside of their space helmets.

Now astronauts inside the space shuttle wear everyday clothes. This lets them do all the things in space that they do on Earth—like scratching their noses.

Rings and Things

People in almost every culture wear jewelry. Metal and stones are worn on earlobes and around necks, fingers, wrists, and arms! Sometimes the jewelry serves a purpose. For example, the Paduang women of Burma stretch their necks by wearing fitted brass rings around them. You might wear a bracelet made of woven threads as a sign of friendship. Jewelry can be as simple as a beaded necklace or as valuable as a diamond.

Colorful jewelry is worn by women in Africa.

Pointy Toes

During the Middle Ages, shoes with pointed toes became very fashionable. The toes of pointed shoes became so long they flapped when a person walked! By the fourteenth century, pointed shoes sometimes went almost 12 inches beyond the wearer's real toes! Poor people were allowed shoes with toes no longer than 6 inches.

Boys in Skirts

As recently as 200 years ago, most boys in Western countries wore full-length skirts! They dressed this way until they were about six years old.

BOYS IN SKIRTS! I THOUGHT IT WAS BAD ENOUGH THAT GIRLS WEAR THEM.

The Ruby Slippers

The famous shoes worn by Dorothy in the movie *The Wizard of Oz* were sold for $165,000 at an auction in 1988. The ruby slippers are size 6B.

All around the world, people celebrate special days in special ways. So let's take a quick trip through the months of the year with Charlie Brown and the *Peanuts* gang and meet some of these great holidays to remember.

HOORAY FOR HOLIDAYS!

CHAPTER 14

A HOLIDAY TRIP THROUGH THE CALENDAR

NEW YEAR'S DAY

VALENTINE'S DAY

EASTER

MAY DAY

Month	Holiday
January	New Year's Day
January or February	Chinese New Year
January	Martin Luther King Day
February	Groundhog Day
February, March or April	Ramadan
February or March	Lent
February or March	Ash Wednesday
February or March	Mardi Gras
February or March	Pancake Day (England)
February	Lincoln's Birthday
February	Valentine's Day
February	Susan B. Anthony Day
February	Presidents' Day
February	George Washington's Birthday
March	Saint Patrick's Day
March or April	Holy Week
March or April	Easter
March or April	Passover
April	April Fools' Day
April	Buddha's Birthday (Japan)
April or May	Arbor Day
May	May Day

Month	Holiday
May	Be Kind to Animals Week
May	Mother's Day
May	Victoria Day (Canada)
May	Memorial Day
June	Flag Day
June	Children's Day
June	Father's Day
June	Jean Baptiste Day (Canada)
July	Canada Day (Canada)
July	Fourth of July
July	Bastille Day (France)
August	Friendship Day
September	Labor Day
September or October	Rosh Hashanah
September or October	Yom Kippur
October	Columbus Day
October	Halloween
November	Guy Fawkes Day (England)
November	Election Day
November	Veterans Day
November	Thanksgiving
December	Hanukkah
December	Christmas
December	Kwanzaa

MOTHER'S DAY

FRIENDSHIP DAY

HALLOWEEN

THANKSGIVING

CHRISTMAS

Put on your party hat and blow up some balloons. The new year is about to begin, and there are lots of holidays coming your way. Let's start with January, February, and March. Away we go with the *Peanuts* gang to celebrate!

SAY HELLO TO THE NEW YEAR

JANUARY

Has New Year's Day always been January 1?

No. Most countries in Europe did not make January 1 the first day of the new year until about 1600. England waited until 1752. Before those dates, the Christian countries of Europe celebrated the new year on March 1 or March 25, at the very beginning of spring.

January 1 was the first day of the new year on the Roman calendar. That calendar was very much like the one we use today. About 45 years before Jesus was born, it was put into use by Julius Caesar (SEEZ-ur). However, the idea of a January 1 new year didn't catch on for hundreds of years.

Why do some people make a lot of noise on New Year's Eve?

Thousands of years ago, people believed that evil spirits roamed the Earth. Because they thought that the spirits were especially dangerous at the new year, people made loud noises at the moment the new year began in order to scare them away.

Most of us don't believe in evil spirits anymore, but we still make loud noises when the clock strikes 12 on New Year's Eve. Blowing horns and shaking rattlers and noisemakers is a lot of fun.

113

When do the Chinese celebrate their new year?

The Chinese New Year begins on a new moon and may occur at any time between January 21 and February 19. It lasts from 10 to 15 days.

The Chinese New Year's Eve and New Year's Day are quiet family days. Then the celebrations get livelier. There are parades almost every day. Musicians, clowns, and dancers in the parades make people laugh.

Colorful dragon floats are paraded through streets to celebrate the Chinese New Year.

How does the Chinese New Year celebration end?

The Chinese New Year celebration ends with the Festival of Lanterns. The Chinese make beautiful lanterns from silk, papier-mâché (PAY-pur muh-SHAY), and glass. They shape some to look like cars, fish, dragons, animals, airplanes, and Chinese houses. The lanterns hang outside houses and in gardens. They hang in front of shops and temples.

When the sky gets dark on the festival day, the people parade with many lanterns. Boys wear fantastic costumes and prance about on stilts. The highlight of the evening is a papier-mâché dragon. It is often as long as a passenger-train car. Sometimes it takes 50 men and boys to carry the dragon.

In the Union of Myanmar, people celebrate the new year by pouring water over their heads!

HAPPY NEW YEAR?

Civil rights leader Dr. Martin Luther King, Jr.

What is Martin Luther King Day?

It is a special day in the United States to remember Martin Luther King, Jr., a famous black American civil rights leader and minister. He worked peacefully to bring about equal rights for black Americans.

The United States honors the memory of Martin Luther King, Jr., on the third Monday in January. This day was chosen so that we may remember this great man on or near his birthday, January 15.

A groundhog peeks out of its burrow.

What happens on Groundhog Day?

According to an old tradition, the groundhog, or woodchuck, wakes up from its winter sleep and comes out of its hole on February 2. If the groundhog sees its shadow, the story goes, it becomes frightened and goes back into its den. This is supposed to mean there will be six more weeks of winter. If the groundhog doesn't see its shadow, it won't be frightened and will stay up to search for food. This is supposed to mean spring will be coming soon.

Both the Germans and the English brought the Groundhog Day tradition to America. For hundreds of years, Germans have watched the badger on February 2. They say the badger's behavior on that day will tell them whether spring is coming early or late. The English have watched the hedgehog for the same reason. German and English settlers in America began watching the groundhog to continue the tradition.

116

What is Lent?

Lent is the time each year when Christians prepare for Easter. It is the 40 days (not counting Sundays) from Ash Wednesday to Easter. The 40 days remind Christians of the time Jesus spent praying and fasting in the desert.

The word *Lent* comes from an old word for spring, *lengthentide*, when the days are lengthening, or growing longer. Lent can start anywhere from February 4 to March 11, depending on when Easter Sunday itself comes.

A long time ago, Christians followed strict rules of fasting during Lent. They did not eat any foods with eggs, milk, meat, or animal fat in them. The rules are less strict today.

Lent is a time when Christians are expected to think about the needs of other people. As a sign of their faith, some people give up a favorite food or activity for 40 days. Sharing what is given up is a chance to help the needy.

Why do some people have ashes on their foreheads on Ash Wednesday?

Christian churches have special Ash Wednesday services at the start of Lent. In some churches, ashes are used to mark small crosses on the foreheads of the people. Ashes are an ancient symbol of sorrow. They remind people to be sorry for their sins.

The ashes used in churches on Ash Wednesday are made by burning the palm branches used on Palm Sunday the year before. Palm Sunday is the Sunday before Easter.

117

What is Mardi Gras?

Mardi Gras (MAR-dee grah) is a festival on the Tuesday before the start of Lent. The Mardi Gras celebration began in France in the 1400s. It is the day that ends a season of parades, parties, and carnivals.

Mardi Gras means "fat Tuesday" in French. It dates from the time when Christians had to use up all animal fat before Lent. From early January until the night before Ash Wednesday, the French people would celebrate. The biggest festival of all was on fat Tuesday.

Today, Mardi Gras carnivals are popular in many European cities. Rio de Janeiro, Brazil, has a carnival, too.

Some Christians call the day before the beginning of Lent Shrove Tuesday. *Shrove* is an old word that means "to confess sins." On Shrove Tuesday people go to church, confess their sins, and then go home for a big party.

Do people in the United States celebrate Mardi Gras?

Yes. French settlers brought the Mardi Gras festival to the United States. Cities in Alabama, Florida, Louisiana, Mississippi, and Texas have colorful Mardi Gras celebrations. The biggest is in New Orleans, Louisiana. Many families of French background still live there. They celebrate with a carnival that lasts for ten days. People come from all over the United States to join the fun. They wear masks and fancy costumes, go to parties and balls, and watch parades. Groups called Krewes sponsor the events. Each Krewe names a king and queen for its parade, a custom dating back hundreds of years to carnivals in Europe.

The biggest parade and parties are on the last day of the carnival. A Krewe called the Rex Organization (*rex* is a Latin word meaning "king") chooses the king of the whole carnival. There is a parade with bands and gigantic floats lit by huge torches. Everyone wears a mask—except the king of the carnival—and dances until dawn.

I'D MAKE THE PERFECT MARDI GRAS QUEEN!

What is Pancake Day?

People in England celebrate Pancake Day on the Tuesday before Lent begins. As we learned, long ago Christians were not supposed to eat fats, milk, and eggs during Lent. In England, people make pancakes to use up those foods.

Children in England like to play toss-the-pancake on Pancake Day. Someone throws a pancake in the air. Children jump up and try to grab it. Whoever catches the biggest piece wins a prize.

In Olney, England, a Pancake Day race takes place every year. Women run carrying frying pans in which pancakes are still cooking!

Do people in the United States celebrate Pancake Day?

The townspeople of Liberal, Kansas, also hold a Pancake Day race. After the race is over, the people of Liberal talk by telephone to the people of Olney, England, to compare winning speeds.

Do all Americans celebrate Lincoln's Birthday?

No. Only 24 states in the United States celebrate Lincoln's Birthday, February 12, as a separate holiday. Eight more states put Lincoln's Birthday and Washington's Birthday together into Presidents' Day. Some southern states don't celebrate Lincoln's Birthday at all because Abraham Lincoln was president during the Civil War. At the start of that war, the South withdrew from the United States. President Lincoln's northern army fought the southern army and brought the South back into the country.

ABRAHAM LINCOLN

119

Who was Saint Valentine?

Nobody knows for sure, and there are several saints named Valentine. One Saint Valentine was a Christian priest who lived in the city of Rome about 300 years after the birth of Jesus. The emperor of Rome refused to allow people to be married in a Christian ceremony. Valentine ignored the emperor and continued to perform marriages in the Christian way. When the Romans found out, they executed Valentine. Later, February 14 became Saint Valentine's Day, a day to honor the priest. Still later, it became simply Valentine's Day, a day for sweethearts.

Why did people begin sending valentines to each other?

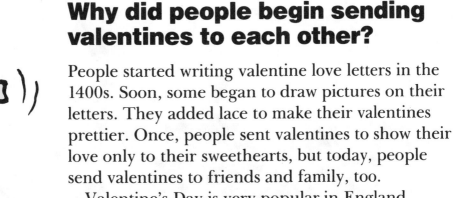

People started writing valentine love letters in the 1400s. Soon, some began to draw pictures on their letters. They added lace to make their valentines prettier. Once, people sent valentines to show their love only to their sweethearts, but today, people send valentines to friends and family, too.

Valentine's Day is very popular in England, France, the United States, and Canada.

In ancient Rome, young men drew women's names out of a box on Valentine's Day. They became sweethearts for a day!

SUSAN B. ANTHONY

When is Susan B. Anthony Day?

People honor Susan B. Anthony on her birthday, February 15. Susan B. Anthony was an American who lived in the 1800s. At that time, women were not allowed to vote in elections. Susan B. Anthony fought very hard to get women that right. In 1872, she voted and was arrested for it. She was found guilty and was fined, but refused to pay. The judge, however, allowed her to go free. When she died in 1906, only four states had given women the right to vote. Today, every woman has that right.

George Washington crossing the Delaware River

When do Americans celebrate George Washington's Birthday?

George Washington was born on February 22, but his birthday is now celebrated on Presidents' Day, the third Monday in February. In this way, many people can enjoy a long holiday weekend. George Washington was the first president of the United States. He was also commander in chief of the army during the American Revolutionary War. Americans fought that war so they could rule their own country. Washington is the only American president whose birthday people celebrated while he was still alive.

MARCH

Why do Irish people celebrate Saint Patrick's Day?

Saint Patrick is the patron saint of Ireland. He introduced Christianity to Ireland. Saint Patrick's Day is both a holy day and a national holiday in Ireland. It is also popular in American cities where many Irish families live. A lot of non-Irish people enjoy the holiday, too. Saint Patrick's Day is March 17, the anniversary of Saint Patrick's death more than 1,500 years ago.

Why do people wear green on Saint Patrick's Day?

Saint Patrick's Day is an Irish holiday, and green has almost always been connected with Ireland. Perhaps this is because the hills of Ireland look so green. There is a legend that says that in Ireland's landscape there are 40 shades of green. In addition, shamrocks, small three-leaved plants, grow wild in Ireland and stay green the year round.

Was Saint Patrick Irish?

No! Saint Patrick wasn't born in Ireland. He was probably born in Wales. He called himself *Patricus*, which is Latin for "well-born." Patricus is Patrick in English.

Saint Patricus went to Ireland as a slave. He had been captured by Irish raiders who knew nothing of Christianity. Later, he escaped and returned to his home, where he became a Christian bishop. He went back to Ireland to teach Christianity to the people there.

On March 28, students in the Czech Republic celebrate Teacher's Day by bringing flowers and gifts to their teachers!

What is Holy Week for Christians?

Holy Week is the week before Easter. It can be in March or April, depending on when Easter falls. It begins on Palm Sunday, when churchgoers receive palm leaves. The palms remind Christians of the time Christ entered Jerusalem and the crowds hailed him as a king by laying palms in his path.

The next important day in Holy Week is Thursday. Called Maundy (from a word in a Latin hymn), it keeps alive the memory of the Last Supper when Jesus introduced Holy Communion. The Last Supper was a Passover meal that Jesus ate with his disciples (dih-SIGH-pulls)—his closest followers.

Good Friday is the saddest day of the year for Christians. On Good Friday, Christians remember the crucifixion (crew-suh-FIK-shun) and burial of Jesus. *Crucifixion* means "being put to death on a cross." The day before Easter is Holy (or Low) Saturday. Churches have no services that day.

Why do Christians celebrate Easter?

Easter is the happiest and most important Christian holy day. On Easter, Christians celebrate their belief in the resurrection (rez-uh-RECK-shun) of Jesus Christ on the third day after his crucifixion. *Resurrection* means "a rising from the dead."

The Christian religion teaches that Jesus' resurrection is a great victory over death. It brings new and everlasting life to all who believe in Jesus.

The English word *Easter* probably comes from *Eostre*, an ancient goddess, whose festival was in the spring. Easter is always in the spring.

Why is the egg an Easter symbol?

In many of the world's cultures, the egg stands for new life. It is from an egg that new life bursts forth. The egg is a reminder to Christians of the resurrection of Jesus and the spiritual life it gives them.

When did people begin to decorate eggs at Easter?

UKRAINIAN EASTER EGGS

No one is certain. Some people think the Egyptians colored eggs in the spring long before Jesus was born. Before dye was invented, people colored eggs by wrapping them in leaves and flowers and dropping them in boiling water. This gave the eggs the color of green leaves or red petals. Later, Christians painted eggs and had them blessed. They gave some to friends on Easter.

Why does the Easter bunny carry colored eggs?

In many cultures, the white rabbit, or hare, like the egg, stands for new life. There are many old stories about hares and eggs.

A German tale says that a poor woman hid colored eggs in a nest. They were an Easter gift for her children. Just as the children saw the nest, a hare hopped away, so people said the hare had brought the eggs. Today, people call the Easter hare the Easter bunny.

IT'S THE EASTER BEAGLE!

A Jewish family at a Passover seder

What is Passover?

Passover is a happy Jewish holiday. It celebrates the Jews' escape from slavery in Egypt more than 3,000 years ago. It is celebrated in March or April, depending on when it falls on the Jewish calendar.

For most Jews, the holiday lasts eight days. During that time, they eat special foods, such as matzo (MOTT-suh), that remind them of their ancestors' escape. Most Jewish families invite their relatives and friends to join them on the eve of the first two days for a *seder* (SAY-dur), a special meal and religious service.

What happens at a seder?

During a *seder*, the Jewish people sit around the dining table and read aloud from a book called the *Haggadah* (hah-GAH-duh). It tells the story of the Jews' slavery and escape to freedom. On the table are a plate of matzos and a plate of special foods: horseradish; parsley or celery; a mixture of wine with crushed apples, almonds, and cinnamon; a lamb's shank bone; and a roasted egg. They are symbols of Jewish slavery and deliverance.

What do the special foods on a Passover table stand for?

Each of the special foods on the *seder* plate stands for something. The horseradish, called *maror* (mah-RORE) in Hebrew, is a bitter herb. It reminds the Jews of the bitterness of slavery in Egypt. It also recalls the bitter fate of those modern Jews who live in countries that don't allow them to follow the laws of their faith.

The parsley or celery, called *karpas* (CAR-pahss), is a reminder of the poor food supply the ancient Jewish slaves lived on. During the *seder* ceremony, a piece of *karpas* is dipped into salt water. The salt water stands for the tears of the slaves.

The wine-apple-almond-cinnamon mixture is called *haroset* (har-OH-set). It represents the mortar, or cement, that the Jewish slaves had to mix as they worked for their Egyptian masters.

The shank bone stands for the lamb that was offered by Jews as a sacrifice to God in the ancient days. The roasted egg, still in its shell, is a symbol of a special sacrifice offered during early Passover celebrations. The egg is called *baitza* (bait-ZAH).

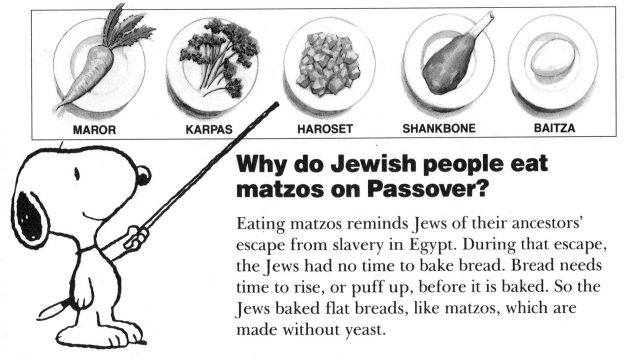

MAROR   KARPAS   HAROSET   SHANKBONE   BAITZA

Why do Jewish people eat matzos on Passover?

Eating matzos reminds Jews of their ancestors' escape from slavery in Egypt. During that escape, the Jews had no time to bake bread. Bread needs time to rise, or puff up, before it is baked. So the Jews baked flat breads, like matzos, which are made without yeast.

127

April, May, and June bring holidays that everyone likes. There's April Fools' Day for kids, Mother's Day for moms, and Father's Day for dads. There's even Be Kind to Animals Week in May—a special time for Snoopy and Woodstock!

A HOLIDAY FOR EVERYONE

BE KIND TO ANIMALS WEEK

APRIL

APRIL FOOLS!

What is the month of Ramadan?

Ramadan (ram-uh-DON) is the ninth month of the Muslim calendar. It begins in April of our calendar year. Muslims, the people of the Islamic (iss-LAM-ick) religion, fast during this month.

During Ramadan, adult Muslims fast from sunrise to sunset. Not only do they *eat* nothing during that time, but they *do* almost nothing as well. All business stops in Muslim countries. Everyone spends the days resting. In the evenings, people get up, join friends and family, and have a big meal and a lot of fun.

How did April Fools' Day get started?

We know that April Fools' Day is the first day of April, but no one is sure how it got started. Most countries seem to have a day when people play tricks. Children especially like these days.

Some people think that trick days began in India. People in India celebrate a spring holiday called the Hindu Festival of the Holi (HOE-lee). A favorite trick on Holi is to fill a bamboo pipe with colored powder and blow the powder at people. Sometimes children fill the pipe with water and squirt one another.

How do Muslims celebrate the end of Ramadan?

They celebrate it with a festival called Id-al-Fitr (EE-dill-FIH-ter). *Id-al-Fitr* means "the fast is over." In the morning, Muslims pray in the mosques (MOSKS), houses of prayer. They return home for a feast—their first midday meal in a month. Noodles cooked with milk, sugar, and coconut are a favorite food on Id-al-Fitr.

For this holiday, Muslims wear new clothes and exchange gifts. They enjoy fairs, carnival rides, and fireworks displays that last for three days.

Muslims in prayer

How do people in Japan celebrate Buddha's birthday?

People in Japan celebrate the birthday of Buddha (BOO-duh) with a flower festival on April 8. Buddha was a great religious leader in India. He lived about 500 years before Jesus was born. He taught people to be peaceful, generous, and kind to one another. In that way, he said, they could find true happiness. His followers spread his teachings throughout Asia.

On Buddha's birthday, millions of Japanese Buddhists go to their neighborhood temples carrying fresh flowers. There, they wash a small statue of Buddha with sweet tea. Little girls cover their faces with white powder so that they will look clean and fresh for Buddha. Children wear silk

Statue of Buddha in Kamakura, Japan

kimonos (robes) decorated with fresh flowers. Buddhist priests march through the streets wearing costumes of olden days. Many floats pass by in a parade. One float always carries a statue of Buddha on a huge white elephant. In India, only important royalty were allowed to ride on white elephants.

WELL DONE, WOODSTOCK!

What is Arbor Day?

Arbor Day is a special day for planting trees. The first Arbor Day celebration in the United States took place in Nebraska on April 10, 1872. On that day, people in Nebraska planted a million trees.

Some holidays celebrate the past, but Arbor Day is dedicated to the future. Trees prevent floods and keep topsoil from blowing away. A tree is the symbol of life in many cultures.

Although the first Arbor Day was celebrated in April, there is no set date for it in the United States. Many states celebrate it in May.

MAY

What is May Day?

May Day is an ancient holiday on which people welcomed spring by dancing around a large pole hung with streamers. The pole is called a Maypole. May Day is celebrated on May 1 in parts of Europe.

Is there a special time to remember pets?

Yes. In the United States, there is a Be Kind to Animals Week during the first full week in May. During that week, people are reminded to have their pets checked by an animal doctor. They are taught how to take care of their pets.

When did people start celebrating Mother's Day?

Many people in all parts of the country thought that a special day should be set aside for mothers. In 1872, one woman in Boston, Julia Ward Howe, wanted that day to be June 2. In Philadelphia, another woman, Anna Jarvis, wanted to set aside the second Sunday in May to remember mothers, after her own mother died in 1907. In 1914, Mother's Day became a national holiday. Now Americans honor their mothers on the second Sunday in May.

QUEEN VICTORIA OF ENGLAND

Why do the Canadians celebrate Victoria Day?

Canada is part of the British Common-wealth—a group of countries that either are or once were under English rule. Victoria Day celebrates the birthday of Queen Victoria, who ruled England and the Commonwealth for 64 years (1837–1901). After she died, people continued to celebrate her birthday, May 24. Modern Canadians celebrate the holiday on the Monday that comes just before May 25.

How do Americans honor the people who died in wars?

People honor American soldiers who died in wars on Memorial Day. Memorial Day used to be called Decoration Day because people decorated soldiers' graves with flowers. It is celebrated on the last Monday in May.

On Memorial Day, in Washington, D.C., a wreath is placed on the Tomb of the Unknowns. These soldiers died in World War I, World War II, and the Korean War. In this way, the United States honors all its citizens who died in wars. The Vietnam Memorial, inscribed with the names of more than 58,000 soldiers who are dead or missing, pays tribute to the brave men and women who fought in the Vietnam War.

Most southern states have their own Memorial Day, which they celebrate in April or May. On this holiday, southerners remember the Confederate soldiers who fought in the Civil War.

JUNE

When do Americans celebrate Flag Day?

June 14 is Flag Day in the United States. On that day in 1777, leaders of the American colonies voted to accept a new flag as the symbol of their country.

Today the American flag has 50 stars—one for each state.

Before that, they flew the Grand Union flag, which had a small design of the English flag on it. The new flag had 13 stars, to stand for the 13 states.

There is a legend of how a seamstress named Betsy Ross made the first American flag. The story goes that General George Washington wanted the stars to have six points, but Betsy talked him into using five-pointed stars.

Is there a Children's Day?

Yes. Many Protestant churches in the United States celebrate Children's Day on the second Sunday in June. Children in the church take part in religious programs and sometimes are promoted from one Sunday school class to the next.

Throughout history, other countries have celebrated children's days in various ways. One custom sure to please kids is practiced in Turkey. On that country's Children's Day, movies are free, and there are free ice cream and candy for the kids!

HOORAY FOR CHILDREN!

In India, people welcome summer in an unusual way. They throw colored water and powder on each other!

HAPPY SUMMER, CHARLES!

When did Americans begin to celebrate Father's Day?

People in Spokane, Washington, celebrated the first Father's Day in 1910. Louise Dodd, who lived in Spokane, thought that fathers should be honored with a special day that would bring fathers and children closer together. She talked to her minister about it. Then he, a few other ministers, and the YMCA persuaded people to celebrate Father's Day. The idea spread to other states. In 1924, President Calvin Coolidge asked people all over the country to honor their fathers with a special day. Ever since then, Americans have celebrated Father's Day on the third Sunday in June.

Dear Dad, Happy Father's Day! AND ALL THE KIDS SIGNED IT!

6-18

What is Jean Baptiste Day?

Jean Baptiste (ZHON Bah-TEEST)—Saint John the Baptist—is the patron saint of Quebec, a French-speaking city in Canada. People celebrate Jean Baptiste Day with a parade. A favorite float in the parade shows Saint John as a little boy dressed as a shepherd. A lamb with a ribbon and a bow around its neck stands next to him. The lamb stands for Jesus. Great crowds gather in the city of Montreal and cheer little Saint John and his lamb. The Jean Baptiste holiday begins on June 24 and can last for as long as eight days.

CHAPTER 17

Flags fly high, and shimmering colors explode in the sky. It must be Canada Day or the Fourth of July! Come along and celebrate these independence days and many other kinds of holidays, from July right through September.

SUMMER FULL OF HOLIDAYS

JULY

When do Canadians celebrate Canada Day?

Canadians celebrate Canada Day on July 1. This is Canada's birthday. Like the United States, Canada was once ruled by England, but on July 1, 1867, the English decided to make Canada a dominion. A dominion makes its own laws, but it is still loyal to another country that has a king or queen. On Canada Day, which used to be called Dominion Day, Canadians display flags and watch parades. The Canadian mounted police wear bright red jackets!

Why do people in the United States celebrate the Fourth of July?

This painting shows the signing of the Declaration of Independence.

The Fourth of July is the birthday of the United States. In the 1700s, England ruled the 13 colonies along the east coast of what is now the United States. The colonists thought that the English king treated them unfairly. They wanted to rule themselves. In 1776, a group of leaders from the colonies met in Philadelphia to talk about independence from England. Thomas Jefferson wrote their thoughts in a paper called the Declaration of Independence. It said that the colonists wanted to be free, and it told why. The Fourth of July was the day the Declaration of Independence was finished. A new country was born, but it had to fight and win a war with England before it would become a free country.

In Japan, the holiday of Obun is celebrated in July. People who live near water set lanterns on little boats. The lanterns are meant to light the way for returning spirits of dead relatives!

French citizens stormed the Bastille in Paris, July 14, 1789.

Why do the French celebrate Bastille Day?

The Bastille (bas-TEEL) was a French prison to which the French king sent many people who displeased him. On July 14, 1789, French rebels attacked the Bastille, freed the prisoners, and destroyed the prison. The capture of the Bastille by the rebels stands for freedom to the French people. Bastille Day is a great national holiday in France, celebrated with music, parades, parties, and dancing in the streets.

AUGUST

HAPPINESS IS HAVING A FRIEND LIKE YOU!

What is Friendship Day?

In 1919, a greeting card merchant thought a day should be set aside to remember special friends. After all, there were lots of days set aside for other reasons—why not have one to remind us of the people we like best? Congress decided it was a good idea, too, and made the first Sunday in August officially Friendship Day.

September

What is Labor Day?

The United States and Canada both have a day to honor their workers. It is called Labor Day. The word *labor* means "work." Labor Day in both countries is celebrated on the first Monday in September.

> EVEN I WOULD RATHER GO TO SCHOOL!

Labor Day was started in 1882 by Peter McGuire. He was a carpenter who began working when he was 11 years old!

What is Rosh Hashanah?

Rosh Hashanah (ROASH hah-SHAH-nuh) is the start of the Jewish New Year. The words mean "head of the year" in Hebrew. Rosh Hashanah is always in either September or October. Some Jews observe it for one day, but for most it is a two-day holiday. Rosh Hashanah is the beginning of the Ten Days of Repentance (rih-PENT-unts). During these days, Jewish people think about their lives. They repent, or feel sorry about their sins, and look for ways to improve themselves.

On Rosh Hashanah, Jews pray in synagogues (SIN-uh-gogs), Jewish houses of worship. After the service, they have a festive family dinner.

> I'VE MADE THIS LIST OF WAYS IN WHICH YOU COULD IMPROVE YOURSELF, BIG BROTHER.

How do Jews observe Yom Kippur?

Yom Kippur (yom ki-POOR), or the Day of Atonement, is the most sacred day of the Jewish year. It is the day on which Jews atone, or make amends with God, for their sins of the year just past. It marks the end of the Ten Days of Repentance. Jews who are 13 years of age and older fast on Yom Kippur. They do not eat or drink anything for a whole day. The day begins at sunset on Yom Kippur and ends just after sundown the next day.

On the eve of Yom Kippur, the synagogue service begins with the chanting of a prayer of repentance, Kol Nidre (COAL nid-RAY). Many Jews spend the rest of the evening and most of the next day praying in synagogues. Yom Kippur ends at sundown with the blowing of the *shofar* (show-FAR).

A man blowing a *shofar*

What is a shofar?

A *shofar* is a musical instrument made from a ram's horn. It sounds something like a trumpet or a few oboes being played together. The *shofar* that Jews used thousands of years ago could be heard for miles. Sometimes it warned people of danger. It also told people when to go to the temple to pray. The modern *shofar* is smaller and not as loud. Jewish people listen to the sound of the *shofar* on Rosh Hashanah and Yom Kippur. It reminds them to think seriously about their lives.

On Rosh Hashanah, people eat pieces of apple dipped in honey—sweet food to start off a sweet year!

CHAPTER 18

WRAP IT UP!

October, November, and December—here we come! The year is drawing to a close, but the celebrations go on. Halloween and Thanksgiving are just two end-of-the-year favorites for you to enjoy. Then it'll be time to help Charlie Brown and the *Peanuts* gang wrap up the year. Happy holidays!

TO CHUCK

TO CHARLES

OCTOBER

Christopher Columbus landed at San Salvador in the Bahamas, October 12, 1492.

Why do people in the Americas celebrate Columbus Day?

The day honors Christopher Columbus, who landed in America on October 12, 1492. Many people say that Columbus was not the first European to discover America. The Irish and Norwegians claim their explorers came to America first, but no one paid much attention to those discoveries. Columbus's discovery made Europeans realize that a new land, America, existed.

Columbus didn't know that he'd discovered America. He thought he'd landed near China or Japan!

Why do people celebrate Halloween?

Halloween is a combination of holidays that is celebrated on October 31. As a night of ghosts and witches, it was started by the Celts (SELTS). They were people who lived in France and the British Isles hundreds of years ago.

The Celts had a holiday on October 31, called Samhain (SAH-win), which meant "end of summer." So Samhain was a festival marking the end of the food-growing season. The Celts believed that spirits of the fruits and vegetables, and also the ghosts of people, visited the Earth on Samhain. The Celts lit huge bonfires on hilltops to scare the ghosts away.

Years later, the Celts became Christians. They and other Christians celebrated Allhallows (now called All Saints' Day) on November 1. It was a day to remember important Christians who had died. The Celts gave the name Allhallows Eve, or holy evening, to October 31, the night before Allhallows Day. Allhallows Eve was later shortened to "Halloween."

How did trick-or-treating get started?

Trick-or-treating began in Ireland. People went from house to house and begged for food on Halloween. They promised good luck to those who gave and bad luck to those who didn't.

In the Isle of Man, an island off the coast of England, Halloween used to be called Thump-the-Door Night because young boys would pound on doors with turnips and cabbages until someone gave them money to go away!

Who was Jack-o'-Lantern?

To the Celts, Jack-o'-Lantern was the spirit of the pumpkin. The Celts carved a pleasant-looking pumpkin face to show Jack as a good spirit, not a nasty one. The Irish claim that Jack-o'-Lantern was a person who couldn't get into heaven because he was too stingy. The devil didn't want him, either. So ever since, he's had to wander about carrying a lantern. The Irish had no pumpkins, so they made Jack-o'-Lanterns from turnips and potatoes.

Carving pumpkins into Jack-o'-Lanterns is a Halloween tradition.

GOOD GRIEF! I THOUGHT YOU WERE A CAT!

The largest pumpkin in the world, grown in 1992 in Puyallup, Washington, weighed 827 pounds!

Why do people wear spooky costumes on Halloween?

The custom of wearing spooky costumes on Halloween began with a group of Irish Celts called Druids. The Irish believed that evil spirits roamed on Halloween. The Druids wanted to fool the evil spirits into thinking that they were evil spirits, too, so they dressed as ghosts and goblins.

I THINK THAT REAL GHOSTS DON'T WEAR GLASSES, MARCIE!

Is there really a Great Pumpkin?

Not even Linus can answer that question—and he's been waiting for years for the Great Pumpkin to show up!

TRICK OR TREAT

TRICK OR TREAT

NOVEMBER

Why do people in England celebrate Guy Fawkes Day?

On Guy Fawkes Day, November 5, people celebrate the capture of an English traitor named Guy Fawkes. In 1605, he and some friends planned to blow up the Houses of Parliament with the king inside. Parliament is something like the Congress of the United States. The plot was discovered, however, before

any damage was done. Guy Fawkes and his helpers were arrested and executed.

The English celebrate Guy Fawkes Day with mischief-making and a great deal of noise. At night, people march in noisy parades and light firecrackers. Children ring bells, crash cymbals, and bang pots. People stuff a dummy of Guy Fawkes with straw, burn it on top of a large bonfire, and sing and yell while it burns.

Guy Fawkes Day is called Bonfire Night in some parts of England. Originally, bonfires were bone-fires, in which the bones of animals were burned!

When is Election Day?

The Tuesday after the first Monday in November is Election Day in the United States. Every four years, United States citizens vote for a new president and vice president. During other years, they vote for state governors, or city mayors. Sometimes they vote for members of Congress.

In Canada and England, there is no regular national election day. National elections in Canada and England can be called at any time.

How do Americans honor the men and women who served in the armed forces?

On Veterans Day, November 11, Americans honor all men and women who served in the Army, Navy, Marine Corps, and Coast Guard. This holiday was originally called Armistice Day. It was started to celebrate the end of World War I in 1918. On June 1, 1954, its name was changed to Veterans Day.

Canadians have a holiday to honor their citizens who died in wars. It is called Remembrance Day and is celebrated on the same day as Veterans Day.

147

Why do we eat turkey on Thanksgiving Day?

Eating turkey on Thanksgiving is a tradition that started when the Pilgrims ate turkey on the first Thanksgiving. The Pilgrims were a group of English people who came to America in 1620. During their first winter in their new land, they didn't have enough food. Many died, but the next spring, their Native American neighbors taught the Pilgrims to plant corn and gave them many other helpful lessons about farming. By fall, it was clear there would be plenty of food for the next winter.

Because they were thankful, the Pilgrims decided to have a feast with plenty of food—the first Thanksgiving celebration. Their Native American neighbors were invited to the feast, of course.

For the occasion, the Pilgrim men hunted turkeys, which were wild in those days. The tradition lasted, and we eat turkey every year on Thanksgiving Day. Thanksgiving is celebrated in the United States on the fourth Thursday in November. Canada also has a Thanksgiving, observed on the second Monday in October. Both countries celebrate the holiday in the same way.

Why do the Jewish people celebrate Hanukkah?

On Hanukkah (HAH-nuh-kuh), Jews celebrate an event of more than 2,000 years ago. In the second century before Jesus was born, a Greek ruler in Syria had taken over the Jewish land where Israel is now. He had also taken over the Jews' temple in Jerusalem. For three years, the Jews fought until they won back their temple and some of their land.

The Jews wanted to relight their temple lamps, but there was only enough holy oil for one day. A legend says a miracle happened. The lamps were lit, and a tiny bit of oil burned for eight days.

Hanukkah comes during the month of December. Jews celebrate it for eight days in memory of the eight days that the oil burned.

How do Jewish people celebrate Hanukkah?

Every night of Hanukkah, Jews light candles and recite special festival blessings. The Hanukkah candleholder is called a *menorah* (muh-NOR-uh). A *menorah* has space for nine candles—one for each night of Hanukkah plus a *shammash* (shah-MASH), or a serving candle. On the first night, one candle is lit. On the last night, all the candles are lit.

During Hanukkah, Jews eat special holiday foods, usually cooked in oil. Many eat potato pancakes called *latkes* (LAHT-kuz). They sing songs and exchange gifts. Children receive money called Hanukkah *gelt*. Sometimes they also get pieces of chocolate wrapped in gold foil that look like gold coins. They have fun playing with a top called a *dreidel* (DRAY-dill).

SLOW DOWN, WOODSTOCK. WATCHING YOU SPIN ON A DREIDEL IS MAKING ME DIZZY!

When did people begin to celebrate Christmas?

No one knows the day and month of Jesus' birth. It was a long time before Christians set a date for celebrating Christmas. About the year 334, a church in Rome decided Christ's Mass, a church service marking the birth of Jesus, should be on December 25. This custom became popular, and people called Christ's Mass "Christmas."

Who decorated the first Christmas tree?

No one knows for sure, but the custom of bringing an evergreen tree indoors and decorating it at Christmas started in Germany. One legend says that Martin Luther started the practice. Luther was an important Christian leader. According to the story, he noticed the starlit sky through the trees as he walked home one Christmas Eve in the early 1500s. He thought the stars looked as if they were shining on the branches. When he arrived home, Martin Luther placed a small fir tree inside his house and decorated it with lighted candles.

Decorating Christmas trees became popular in Germany. Prince Albert, the German husband of Queen Victoria, brought the tradition to England. Both German and English people brought it to America, where people of many nationalities continued the tradition.

The tallest cut Christmas tree was a Douglas fir that was 221 feet tall! It was set up in a shopping center in Seattle, Washington, in 1950!

Did people always sing Christmas carols?

Christmas has had its own music and songs since it started, but Christmas carols have a special history. The word *carol* means "circle dance." Among many ancient people, caroling was common at festivals. Groups would dance arm-in-arm, often singing simple, happy songs. Carols became a way for Christians to express Christmas joy.

Christmas carols were known in England by the year 1100. Saint Francis of Assisi (uh-SEE-zee), who lived in Italy about 800 years ago, encouraged the singing of Christmas carols. He is sometimes called the Father of the Christmas Carol.

153

What special game do Mexican children play at Christmas?

They like to break piñatas (peen-YAH-tuhs), clay pots that Mexicans make in many shapes. Sometimes a piñata looks like a fat person, a clown, an animal, or Santa Claus. It is filled with Christmas treats such as candy, nuts, and small gifts.

Someone hangs the piñata from the ceiling or a doorway, just above the children's reach. A leader blindfolds the children one at a time, leads each child to the piñata, and gives him or her a stick. The child takes three swings at the piñata while the other children circle around it, dancing and singing. When the piñata breaks, everyone scrambles for the Christmas treats.

Who was the first Santa Claus?

Many people say that Nicholas, the bishop of Myra, was the first Santa Claus. Nicholas lived about 300 years after Jesus was born in what is now part of Turkey. Very little is known about him, but he is supposed to have loved children and to have given them presents.

Nicholas became a popular saint in Europe. He is the patron saint of Russia. His special day is December 6. *Santa Claus* is English for *Sinterklass*, the Dutch name for Saint Nicholas.

Have people always believed that reindeer pull Santa's sleigh?

No. Through the years people have believed many different stories about how Santa Claus travels. Some people have believed that Santa travels on a donkey or a horse. Others have believed that he travels across the sky in a chariot pulled by horses. People who live in Scandinavian countries have always been certain that Santa travels in a sleigh pulled by reindeer. How else could he travel through icy northern Europe?

What is a Yule log?

A Yule log is a big log of wood that some people burn on Christmas Eve. Before the time of Jesus, Scandinavians had a holiday called Yule. They celebrated Yule at the time of year when people today celebrate Christmas. On Yule, they lit huge logs. The fires were supposed to make the sun shine brighter. After Scandinavians became Christians, they continued to burn Yule logs. The custom of burning Yule logs at Christmas spread throughout Europe, including England.

What's the best holiday of the year?

Everybody has his or her own favorite holiday. Snoopy likes Easter because he gets to play the role of the Easter Beagle. Lucy likes April Fools' Day. She enjoys fooling Charlie Brown. Charlie Brown doesn't like any holidays. They remind him of the cards he never gets!

DID YOU KNOW...?

ALOHA!

KAMEHAMEHA

● Kamehameha (kah-may-hah-MAY-hah) Day in Hawaii is the only holiday in the United States that honors royalty. King Kamehameha was born in the early 1700s and died in 1819. He united all the islands of Hawaii into one kingdom. On June 11, Hawaiians hold pageants and parades in King Kamehameha's honor. Flower garlands called leis (LAYZ) are placed on the king's statue in Honolulu.

● Your birthday is important, too! In many places, it's traditional to have a birthday cake with a candle for each year on it. It's good luck to blow out all the candles with one breath. In some countries, children are often named after saints. Each saint has a special feast day, and people celebrate on their saint's day. If your name is Ann, you celebrate on July 26; Saint David's day is March 1.

HEY, RED BARON! SURPRISE! HAPPY BIRTHDAY!!

It's not that kind of Boxing Day, sir!

• People in Mexico celebrate the Days of the Dead on the first and second of November. On those days, the spirits of the dead are welcomed back to Earth for a "visit." Mexicans are very busy before this holiday. They buy new dishes, candlesticks, skeleton dolls, special breads, and candy made in spooky shapes. On October 31, everybody stays up all night, decorating altars with flowers and candles. Cookies, candies, and toys are left on the altar for the souls of children. A special meal is prepared in honor of all the returning souls. Neighbors visit each other and talk about the people they are honoring.

• Some people can celebrate their birthdays only once every four years. February has 28 days in the month, except on leap year, when it has 29 days. If you were born on February 29, you have to wait four years for each birthday! This is because we use a calendar that should have 365 and one quarter days in each year. To make the year an even number of days, we pretend the year is 365 days long for three years, and 366 days long for the fourth year—leap year!

• In December, African-Americans remember their heritage when they celebrate Kwanzaa.

• Boxing Day has nothing to do with people punching one another. Many years ago in England, people gave their servants gifts or "boxes" on the day after Christmas. Today on Boxing Day, December 26, people give gifts to letter carriers and other workers.

Imagine having a birthday party only once every four years!

There's much more to discover in Snoopy's World.
If you've enjoyed *People and Customs of the World*
you'll want to read...

How Things Work

Creatures, Large and Small

Earth, Water and Air

Land and Space